Spíləx̣m

A Weaving of Recovery, Resilience, and Resurgence

NICOLA I. CAMPBELL

HIGHWATER
PRESS

Conseil des arts   Canada Council
du Canada   for the Arts

We acknowledge the support of the Canada Council for the Arts.
Nous remercions le Conseil des arts du Canada de son soutien.

HighWater Press gratefully acknowledges the financial support of the Province of Manitoba through the Department of Sport, Culture and Heritage and the Manitoba Book Publishing Tax Credit, and the Government of Canada through the Canada Book Fund (CBF), for our publishing activities.

HighWater Press is an imprint of Portage & Main Press.
Printed and bound in Canada by Friesens
Design by Jennifer Lum
Cover and interior art by Carrielynn Victor

Library and Archives Canada Cataloguing in Publication
Title: Spílexm : a weaving of recovery, resilience, and resurgence / Nicola I. Campbell.
Names: Campbell, Nicola I., author. Description: Includes index.
Identifiers: Canadiana (print) 20200399535 | Canadiana (ebook) 20200399748 | ISBN 9781553799351 (softcover) | ISBN 9781553799702 (EPUB) | ISBN 9781553799719 (PDF)
Subjects: LCSH: Campbell, Nicola I. | LCSH: Indigenous women—British Columbia—Biography. | LCSH: Indigenous authors—British Columbia—Biography. | LCGFT: Autobiographies.
Classification: LCC PS8605.A5475 Z46 2021 | DDC C818/.603—dc23

24 23 22 21   1 2 3 4 5

HIGHWATER
PRESS

www.highwaterpress.com
Winnipeg, Manitoba
Treaty 1 Territory and homeland of the Métis Nation

For my cǝceʔ, Steffanie Michel.

Table of Contents

❧ Nɬeʔkepmxcín Lullaby

❧ Land Teachings

❧ Coming to My Senses

✿ sorrow

✿ yémit and merímstn

❦ this body is a mountain, this body is the land

❦ Resurgence

Prairie Letters

February 4, 1973
Big River, Sask

Dear Sis,

We're renting this little house in Big River for $25. It's a two-room
place plus a porch. No running water, bathroom. We got some
furniture though. So it's all okay. At least it's a place to stay.
That film that I took of the girls I put in to get developed. So as
soon as we get it out I'll send you a picture. That reminds me
I'm learning how to crochet. It sure is easier than knitting. I'm
going to crochet a throw-over for our couch, when we get a
couch. No radio or television.

So far we've been lucky. I guess about a week before we came it was
about -40 now it's about +20.
Not much more to say except hi to everyone.
Write back.

> All my love
> > Your sis,
> > & John
> > & Nikki

April 5, 1973

Hi Sis,

So how are you and your family. Would you believe it is Nicola's
5th month birthday today.

Would you believe also that it is snowing again. I thought it was
spring. I phoned Dad about two weeks ago. Dad was going to
go to Seattle to pick up Marv's car. Bro is working in Kitchican
(spelling?) Alaska.

I sent dad two pics of Nikki. First thing he says is that she sure
has a lot of hair.

It sure gets boring up here in this ¼ horse town. The most exciting
thing I do during the day is take ½ block walk to the P.O. and
check the mail.

Did you know that Patty lost two of her kids, including one she
adopted, in a house fire. Mom is living with her now.

How do you spell Kitchican. I'd like to write to Bro.

Love your sis.

July 1, 1973
Box 818
Querel Gravel & Lumber
Hudson Bay, Sask

Dear Sis,

Thanks for the dress for Nikki. The little brat is sure getting
around. She can crawl from one end of the trailer to the other
and stand up by grabbing on and walk holding onto the couch.
Little fart isn't even 8 mo yet.

John shot his first moose about a week and a half ago. He sure
was surprised. When he first seen it he thought it was a horse.
We were on our last package of meat and if we wanted any we
had 60 miles to the store. He shot it with a single shot 22. Must
of shot it about 17 times after the first hit before it died. He got it
right on the spine.

Our trailer has 2 bedrooms, a bathroom, kitchen and a living
room. Right now we have no running water or sewer. We have
to get a pressure pump and John has to dig a sewer.

For the first time John brought me some flowers yesterday. Some
wild tiger lilies. Real pretty. Do you suppose it's love?

I'm putting money away for a sewing machine. So far I've got
$25. Last weekend we went to P.A. and looked at sewing machines.

Whew! I was hoping for one like Moms but they are about $250–$500. So I have to settle for one that just does straight and zigzag. Which is about $100.

When you come out if you go to P.A. first, from there you go east towards Nipawin. On the same road you go towards Carrot River, 18 miles until you get to a junction. Keep going on the Shoal Lake road.

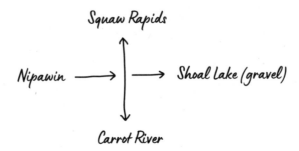

It's gravel. You go 68 miles up the road. You see a sign about 50(?) miles up the road Shoal Lake 2. We are 15 miles past. There's a sign outside camp, Querel Gravel & Lumber. From the road you can't see the camp. But we're only a 100 yds or so in. We're the green and white trailer, beside a small silver one. If my flowers grow we've got flowers on the outside. After all these instructions you better come.

All my love, your sis.

Hi to Don and Suzie. Give little Suzie a kiss for me.

July 26, 1973

they are on a hillside.
baby on a blanket,
nine months old.

a thousand people,
Saskatchewan River.
this is Batoche,
july 26, 1973.

she calls when she sees two children
bobbing like buoys,
swift currents unyielding.

"John, those children are drowning!"

Daddy brought the children to shore
but he did not bring himself.
the river would not set him free.

activist
revolutionary
Woodland Cree
scottish

french
Michif

fiddles
red river jig

the Saskatchewan River
flowed through his veins.

Johnny Campbell was my daddy.
he was Métis.

Her Blood Is From Sptétkʷ

sptétk^w

swells of ċəłetk^wu   cold water
cold, cold water,
joining transforming reforming
rivers like sisters
singing, clear and cold.

synk̇y̓ép sings   coyote
through the valley
across mountains
to the prairies.

she's a Shuta, that one.   Séwtaʔ family name
her blood is from sptétk^w   "Springs" traditional place name
"the place where fresh water
flows up from underground."

nłeʔkepmx   Thompson Interior Salish people
syílx   Okanagan Interior Salish people
scw̓éxmx   "People of the Creeks"

sagebrush and fir boughs,
juniper and wild roses
weave through her veins.

fried bologna and rice

at Auntie's house
we soak hides in the river,
soften them
in brains until they stink.

peee-yew!

then string them up,
stretched and tanned
in smoke.

fried bologna and rice
is a feast
at Auntie's house.

we three snúṅk'ʷe scmém'iʔt   friends / children (pl)
we three childhood friends
drink freshie.

freshie, fried bologna
and rice and
Auntie's fry bread
has two holes in it,

one for me,
one for you.

Auntie always wears her hat
covered with buttons and pins,
angels, turtles, and

bingo!

she sits in the corner by her lamp,
with scissors she cuts her hide,

snip, snip, snnnip!

we three snúṅkʷe scmém'iʔt
we work hard at Auntie's house,
making bread,
making pies,
beading flower necklaces.

yellow house

fall and winter, spring and summer,
mommy dances on a chair as mice run around.
i sit on the potty looking down
while frogs sing from underground.

yellow house, yellow house warm and safe.
Great-Grandpa brought it piece by piece
budda-bump budda-bump on horse and wagon
from nwéyc to sptétkʷ   place names
"a real long time ago."

yellow house, yellow house inside and out,
a-frame roof and attic
wooden cupboards, wooden floors,
wooden ledges, wooden porch.

frame, brace, and two-by-four,
nails, screws, and paint.
root cellar, yúxkn, chicken coop,   storage shed
red barns and corrals across the road.

Great-Grandpa built them all.

children be careful as you play,
be careful as you run through the doorway.
there's a wood stove in the middle
and that fire is burning bright.

Speed Sew

"Where'd Mommy go?" I am in the doorway of my goddaddy's bedroom. Sometimes I stay with my young mom, sometimes I stay with my aunties, and sometimes I stay with my godparents. I love staying with my godparents, but I'm only allowed to stay if they aren't drinking. Next to my young mommy, my godmommy is my favourite person in the whole wide world.

"I don't know where she is, Baby. Go look in her bedroom."

"Hmph." I turn and march back through the kitchen. One Cent, our fat old Siamese cat, is sprawled across the living room floor licking her paws, tail twitching. My godparents have four dogs: Noopy is black, Tina is light brown, and both are Chihuahuas; Lady looks like she's from the movie *Lady and the Tramp*; Tiny is our lassie dog, and he stays outside. They always sit right beside my mommy, unless I'm home. But I can't find any of them. My godmommy bought a brand-new tube of Speed Sew from the fabric store in town and I want to Speed Sew something. If you don't know, Speed Sew is a special glue used for sewing fabric together really fast. Her bedroom door is closed. I turn the doorknob, but the door won't move.

"Mommy? Are you in there?" Noopy yips in response. I call my godmommy "Mommy," too. People always get confused. So everywhere we go, I have to explain that I have two moms: a young mom and a mom who is an Elder. I trace the wood grain with my finger and find the Grandmother and Grandfather faces there. I see them everywhere: in patterns on the tile floor or ceiling, in trees and dirt, in shadows, and even in my mush. Danny's room is right next door.

I stand in his doorway with my toes and my nose inside. I'm not allowed in Danny's room when he's not home. Danny's my godbrother and he's a teenager. He wears Wrangler jeans and a western belt, and he competes in high school rodeos. He has tiny paints and soft paintbrushes, triangle banners on his ceiling, neatly organized stacks of records, and a record player. My favourite songs are "My White Bicycle" and "This Flight Tonight" by Nazareth.

My goddaddy and Danny do steer roping at Indian rodeos too. They're fast and strong on their horses. When we travel, we pack the day before and load the horse trailer and horses right before we head out of town, leaving lonely dogs and a trail of dust at home. The rodeo grounds are a hubbub of activity: cowgirls and cowboys with their horses tied to horse trailers; the crowd cheering for the clown; anxious calves and bulls waiting in the corrals. I'm *this close* to painting at Danny's desk when I hear my godmommy's voice through the closed door.

"Yes, Babygirl."

"What you doing?" Her dresser drawer is scraping closed.

"I'll be out in a few minutes, go play." I stare at the painted door.

"But I don't want to! I want to come in there." I shake the doorknob. She slid the butter knife under the doorframe to lock the door closed, I just know it. Noopy starts to whine.

"I'll be out soon. Noopy, sit down."

"Mommy! I want to come in right now!" Danny's paints don't matter anymore. I shake the knob again. "I wanna Speed Sew too!" I hear the tinkle of Noopy's bell and the clickety-clack of his claws on the floor. Then he's whining and scratching at the door too.

"Not right now, Baby. After. Mommy's busy, go play."

"No, I don't want to play!" Why won't she let me in? Since when?

"Let me in!" I turn the knob, bang hard with my fist balled up tight. "Mommy!" I holler and frown at the Grandmother and Grandfather faces on the door, then slide to the floor. I start crying the blues and Noopy joins me from the other side of the door. Finally, the bed squeaks and the door swings wide and she's standing there. My godmommy has one blue eye and one brown eye, and her auburn hair is in a long, wispy braid. She likes to wear slacks and sweaters.

"Come in, then." I stand up and walk into her room wiping tears from my eyes. Tina and Lady, those traitors, are lying on her bed. Noopy dances at my feet, licking my hands. I wipe his tears and hug him. We're both happy.

Mommy always keeps a clean house, but her bedroom is another story. Her dressers are overflowing. She has things stacked everywhere: coats, bras, dresses, blouses on hangers and stacked on chairs, two holy bibles and jewelry boxes on her dresser. She has a drawer loaded with tiny, mini lipsticks and jewelry: clip-on rhinestone earrings, rhinestone necklaces, and rosaries. Mary the virgin and jesus christ stand in solemn solidarity on her walls.

"Whatcha doing?" On her bed I see the Speed Sew, along with some foam, and a big pair of silver and black scissors. This is exactly where I want to be.

"You just never mind. I'm busy."

"I wanna Speed Sew something. I like Speed Sew. I want some of that." I point to the foam. She has a pink quilt and her bed is neatly fixed. The door is closed, and the butter knife is back in place. Noopy curls up beside me and I get right to work. Mommy draws circles on the foam with a black felt pen. Then she cuts the circles out with her black and silver scissors. My young mom is always busy doing things with her hands, too. She likes to crochet and sew with her sewing machine. She's been gone for a while now. I feel the thickness expand in my throat; my eyes well and my chest is heavy. "When is my real mommy coming back, Mommy?"

"Hmm? She'll come back soon, Babygirl. She always comes back." I try not to feel sad. She's still in the hospital because something happened. Something happened to her and she's all bandaged up. I try not to worry but I always worry about both of them. They both had long hair, but now my young mom's hair is all gone.

My godmommy goes to the hospital too sometimes. One time her wrists were in bandages and she had tubes attached to her nose and arm. She takes medicine from the doctor every day. Sometimes she takes too much. My godmommy always says, "If it wasn't for you, Babygirl, I wouldn't be here." I wonder and wonder, what do those words mean? I don't like the hospital.

I use the black pen and scissors and cut my foam into circles too. Then I Speed Sew them together. She glues foam circles to the inside of a pair of brand-new stretchy panties, the kind with the girdle that holds her tummy in. Speed Sew is rolled up in gooey balls all over my fingers. When I look up, she's wearing those stretchy panties and the foam makes her bum huge. Then she pulls on her slacks. She stands in front of the mirror looking at it from side to side.

"Holy cow! Mommy!" I point at her huge, brand-new bum and poke the squishy foam.

"Ah! You! Don't you even look at me!" Her face is a shade of red I've never seen before. She sits down and tugs them off. "Go on now! You go play!"

hamburger stew

coffee pot perking, tea kettle warm,
framed photo on the wall
of a sailor girl dressed in navy blue.

chop, chop, chop—celery, carrots, onions,
hamburger and potatoes
sizzle in the cast iron pan
on a black and white cookstove.

"Babygirl, sing your bluebird song.
it's good to sing while you cook."

perched on a stool with my wooden spoon,
blue flames dance on low.
she exits the kitchen and i sing.

bluebird, bluebird flying in the sky.
bluebird, bluebird flying really high.

knock, knock, knock!
old-style syílx cowboy drawl, "coffee on?"
Grandpa Adam walks in wearing
chaps, cowboy hat, and western boots.
"yes sir! and Babygirl is cooking hamburger stew!"

cigarette-stained hands, spittoon close by,
nsyílxcn weaves through the house
cowboy coffee and Red Rose tea.
teaspoons sing, "ting ting ting"

lil' dishwasher
nsyílxcn word catcher
i listen, eager to understand
with bubbles on my hands.

lullabies

so many nights i sat awake
and listened.

Old Mom, you were speaking
nɬeʔkepmxcín, nsyílxcn
with the many old ones
who came through our door.

i sat quietly, sometimes.
sometimes i pestered you
with questions.

belly warm with toast,
Red Rose tea, Pacific cream
and sugar.

i sat tracing salt and pepper designs
with my fingers on the
red and white tablecloth,
black and white benches.

listening carefully to grandmother voices,
stories only heard in the quiet hours
between Elders.

"my girl, go to bed!"
"Babygirl, you're asking too many questions!"

nɬeʔkepmxcín
nsyílxcn
english

i could never decide when one ended
and the next began,
lulled to sleep by an Indian lullaby.

your voice soothing,
singing, praying
gently explaining.

"when it is your time, Babygirl,
you will understand."

buckle-up shoes

she'd twirl by herself
in the living room
to the Beatles
and Wanda Jackson,

when she thought no one was watching.

i'd peek around the corner,
maybe four-foot tall
with moccasins on
and wispy braids.

tired out from a day full of
play
i would watch her feet
remember.

in black buckle-up shoes,
a skirt with flare,
a red blouse with a pretty collar,
auburn hair in curls.

Old Mom twirling
like a little girl.

Little People

My young mom said our new house is a CMHC house, but I don't know what CMHC means. I know that it is a program though, that helps single moms buy houses in Canada. It's a pink house. It's about five or ten minutes from Grandpa's house on our reserve and twenty minutes from town. We can't get a house on our reserve because we're non-status. So, I guess it's not our reserve even though our family and ancestors lived in this valley long before the Indian reservations came into existence. The Canadian government took my mom's status away when she married my dad because my dad was Métis from Saskatchewan. So that makes me non-status too because my dad was Métis. It is truly weird that we aren't considered legitimate even though our ancestors are older than the dirt and the rocks and the trees. The Elders say that when the wind blows across the hills throughout this valley, we are breathing the breath of our ancestors, and when we walk, we are walking in the shadows of their footsteps.

My auntie got a CMHC house too; her house is white. It's a couple blocks away from ours. Their house is off-reserve as well because she's married to my uncle and he's non-status from Alberta. After my mom got out of residential school, she eventually moved to Edmonton with Auntie. My mom met my dad at the Edmonton Friendship Centre during the Native rights movement of the 60s and 70s. Apparently, everyone was hitchhiking everywhere during those years. Indigenous people were travelling to participate in Native rights events throughout British Columbia, all across Canada, and down into the United States.

My godmom lives off-reserve even though she has her status. She likes living in town and there aren't enough houses on her reserve. When my young mom was in the hospital, I had to stay in town with my godmom and I stayed with my aunties too. She was in the hospital for three months and that felt like forever. Now my young mom is home, and everything is all better. We live in our brand-new pink house in Lower Nicola, British Columbia.

I walk down the stairs of our house, flipping on light switches all the way down to the basement. Everything is new in this house: the walls, the carpet, the washer and dryer. I don't like the basement, but I do as I'm told. Wet clothes into the dryer, whites into the wash, but the prickles along my skin don't go away. When I turn, there's a thing hanging from the ceiling and a pool of red beneath it on the cement floor. Heart in my throat, I sprint for the stairs. "MOM! Mom! Something is hanging in the basement!" Sliced meat and onions sizzle in her favourite cast iron pan and she's standing by the stove with a fork in her hand.

"Mike and Coot went hunting. It's a deer. It has to hang for a while before it can be butchered."

"A deer? Mike hunted a deer?" Uncle gives us deer meat sometimes, but it's always wrapped in brown paper. We've never had a dead deer in our house before; in fact we've never owned a house before.

"Did you remember to put laundry detergent in the wash?" I shake my head. I don't want to go back down there. She gives me her mom stare. All the blood drains from my face as I retrace my steps back down the stairs. I am not certain which is worse: facing Mom's wrath or facing the dead deer. I try not to stare but I'm afraid not to look. I run to the washer, scoop up a cup of the powdered detergent fast, not taking my eyes off of it.

Hanging from its hind legs, head gone, it is exposed without its hide. Transformation stories from the time of talking animals tell of Coyote taking the skin of other animals and transforming himself in his manipulations of others. You can't really trust synk̓yép, Coyote, because he is always up to trickery and mischief. In the stories that I remember, females young and old should never trust synk̓yép because he likes to take what doesn't belong to him and that includes girls. Stories about when the animals talked are called sptékʷł and I still have a lot to learn about them. I know for a fact that if I wore the deer's hide, I would look nothing like a deer.

When I'm done with the laundry, I stare at the deer, inching closer. I see muscles, sinew, meat, and bone with a pool of blood beneath. I've seen a dead deer on the side of the road before—Mom said it had been hit by a car. I have never been this close to one though. With the tip of my finger I touch flesh and random strands of bristly deer fur. Yesterday, it was alive running through fields of tall grass, fragrant Labrador bushes, and pine trees. Yesterday, it was drinking fresh water from the creek. Now, its antlers are on our wall with pieces of flesh still clinging to them; its front legs curled with the hooves intact. If it could speak, what would it say? When I'm back upstairs I look into the frying pan.

"What's that, Mom?"

"Deer heart and liver, the best parts. Better set the table."

"For who?"

"You know who. The three of us: Mike, me, and you." I look at her for another moment. Her hair is growing long again.

"Okay." I clear and then wipe the kitchen table, all the while contemplating Mike. Mike is Mom's new boyfriend. He is Syílx. An Okanagan Indian from Quilchena, BC. My mom's mom, she would be my grandmother, was Syílx too. We aren't related to him though. The noises below us indicate he's downstairs again, huffing and rumbling around. He has put his tool boxes and things carpenters use down there. When we first moved in, I dreamt the basement was a cave that went deep underground, but it's his workshop now. He's always busy and if he isn't busy, he's sleeping or watching TV. He likes to lie down in front of the television with his feet crossed just like my grandpa does. He has long, wiry black hair that he ties with a buckskin string. I know it's buckskin because I smelled it once when it was on the bathroom counter. I know what buckskin smells like because my Auntie E. I. is always tanning deer hides to make beautiful buckskin moccasins.

When Auntie E. I. is given a deer or moose hide, she either strings it up on a wooden rack and scrapes it clean right away or she puts it in the freezer so that she can process it later. She used to tie it to a tree in order to soak it in the river until one day, we went to check her hide and it was gone. We weren't sure if it was coyotes or high water or dogs from the reserve that took it. She was upset and didn't want animals stealing her hides, so she started soaking them in a barrel covered with a lid. She even put a great big, heavy brick on top to keep it closed. She uses every part of the deer, including the meat, bones, hooves, hide, and a concoction made with the deer brains that helps soften the hide. After that, she strings up the hide on a special wooden rack and lights a smoky fire underneath. The fire can't be too close, or it will burn the hide. She has special tools for scraping, stretching, and tanning her hides.

"It's important to know where your blood comes from, especially because we're related to darn near everyone in the valley." My other-other auntie, my mom's oldest sister, is always reciting a long list of our family bloodlines and who we're related to. My young mom and numerous aunties and relatives have been researching our family tree. My mom comes from a family with nine children, so she has five sisters and three brothers.

"Your maternal grandfather, maternal great-grandparents, and extended family are all Nłeʔkepmx—in the Nicola Valley, we are referred to as Scwéxmx. Your maternal grandmother, her parents and extended family are Syílx from up Fish Lake out towards Vernon, BC." Nłeʔkepmx people are categorized as part of the Interior Salish linguistic group. There are several language groups categorized as Interior Salish: Nłeʔkepmx, Secwepmx, Sx̌ax̌'imx, and Syílx. The traditional territory of the Nłeʔkepmx includes the Fraser Canyon, Boston Bar, Siska, through Spences Bridge up into the Nicola Valley, and all the way over to Hedley and the Similkameen Valley.

"Your Great-Grandma Mem's english name was Lily and Great-Grandpa Pep's english name was Tim. They had twelve children including Grandpa, your mom's dad. Can you imagine all those children and descendants? That is a small part of our family tree. Our family tree shows that, through Mem, we are also descendants of Chief Nk'wala. Chief Nk'wala was a well-known chief from the Nicola Valley. It is important for you to learn your family tree and remember who your family is." Our family is enormous and remembering everyone's name is hard. I'm better at remembering my cousins and my aunties—especially the ones I play with and the ones who take care of me.

Cutlery, dishes, salt and pepper, butter, a little saucer with bread; the table is almost set. That's when I look below the kitchen table for the hole. It's a habit. The one I hate (not Mike) put the hole there when he was drunk. He wrecked the wall in our brand-new house by putting a chair through it. Like in the stories of Coyote's trickery, that man disguised himself as a nice man. He pretended, but when he was drunk, he was mean. I can't help but remember that man every time I see the hole in the wall. I move the chairs around, searching. When I find it, it's covered with a patch of white.

"Hey Mom, look! That hole is gone!"

"Mike patched it."

"Mike patched it?" I look again. Like my knees, the wall has a scar, but the wound is gone. After supper Mike goes downstairs with his knife and a handsaw. He brings up a huge hunk of meat that he calls a hindquarter. And I inspect him, his eyes. The sound of his laugh. I inspect his hands, bloody from working with the deer meat. I watch every move he makes in our kitchen and I can't see anything mean in him, anywhere. Not in his eyes, not in his hands, not in a single strand of his hair or even his chin.

I help wash dishes while they butcher the meat on the kitchen table for stew, roasts, steaks, and stir-fry. They even have a silver contraption that they attach to the counter. They stuff hunks of meat in the top, turn a metal crank and meat comes out the bottom like soft ice cream.

In the morning, Mom cooks pancakes, eggs, and bacon for breakfast and we all sit at the table and eat together all over again: my mom, Mike, and me. His name is Mike, but everyone calls him Brown or even Mr. Brown. And when he teases my mom too much, she calls him, "Michael Brown." Brown isn't his real name; it's a nickname, but it's a good one for him. He's quiet and his voice is gentle. He would definitely be a brown bear, I know it. He huffs around the house like a bear, especially when he's downstairs in his workshop. Mr. Brown built a shelf using grey bricks for his stereo. He likes a radio station from Vancouver called *99.3 The Fox*. We listen to George Thorogood, The Animals, Tina Turner, The Beatles, whatever happens to be playing on *The Fox*. Or we listen to records.

After the breakfast dishes are done, Mom gets into her Sunday cleaning vibe because every Sunday is cleaning day. His radio station is still playing but I can't find Mr. Brown. He's not lying on the couch with his feet crossed. He's not downstairs in his workshop area, where he hung the deer. He's not in their bedroom. They share my mom's bedroom because he lives with us now. I used to be able to sleep with her, especially when I had bad dreams, but not anymore. He's nowhere inside the house. I walk to the back door and stand on the back deck. He's starting a little garden for his special plants, right behind the house, but he's not there either. I come back inside.

"Mom, where's Mike?" She's washing every single windowsill in the whole house. She lifts a living room window and then pulls it right out of the frame. She doesn't answer so I ask again, "Mom, where's Mike?"

"He went for a walk."

"Where?"

"Up there." She points out the window towards the mountains. "Help me clean the windows." She hands me the Windex and paper towels. Ever since she got this new house, all she wants to do is clean. Not just a little bit either; she scrubs everything.

"Up the mountains?" I was mystified. "Who did he go with?" Clear blue liquid runs in streams down the glass.

"He went alone."

"What's he doing?" I unravel a huge wad of paper towel and wipe.

"I don't know, walking. Don't waste the paper towel."

"Did he bring a gun? Is he hunting again? Maybe Coot is with him." I look at her and her eyebrows are raised, so I pull a couple pieces from my wad and use only them. When they're saturated, I grab two more.

"He's fine." She's annoyed so I stop asking questions.

"That's weird, Mom." I keep looking out the window. "Is he just walking around the mountain?" The hayfields roll and gradually rise into the mountainside, which is covered in pine trees and juniper. When I'm finished washing windows, I mop the kitchen floor, the bathroom floor, and the landing. When I am finished mopping, Mom says it's still sticky, so I have to mop it all over again. A clean house is good until I have to clean, too.

"Mom, when's Mike coming home?" The fridge and stove are clean, the windows and windowsills are clean, and the living room is vacuumed with her brand-new vacuum. Now she's digging around in her sewing kit. Fabric and denim squares are heaped in stacks on the table and there is deer meat cooking in the oven. I can smell it.

"I don't know. He must be hungry by now." She pauses. "Unless he packed a bologna sandwich."

Mmmm, a bologna sandwich. "I wonder how far he'll walk?"

"I don't know. He must have made it past the dump by now."

"Really?" I was in shock. That was a long walk in the mountains. All by himself.

"Yes, I wouldn't be surprised. He's probably looking at things."

"In the dump or up the mountains?"

"Both."

"I wonder if he found a cave." It would be so cool if Mr. Brown found a cave that went deep inside the mountain. I remember Elders talking about the Little People. I wonder what they look like? I wonder what kind of house they live in? Little People must make their canoes out of leaves. Maybe they live in pit houses like our ancestors did. I wonder what it was like to live in a pit house. In our language, the word for pit house is s?ístkn. "Mom! Do you think he'll see Little People when he's in the mountains?"

"What? The little who?" She is busy with one of her sewing projects now. She has her special case for head pins and is surrounded by a multitude of square pieces of fabric in different colours and designs. Her treasured electric sewing machine is close by.

"You know, the Little People." I raise my eyebrows as if to say, "duh" but I don't say it out loud because if I did, I'd be in big trouble.

"Oh for goodneth thaketh! He'll be home thoon. Go clean your room." She's speaking with a lisp because she has head pins between her teeth. She is preparing to sew her first row of squares for a brand-new patchwork quilt. I look at her and run for my shoes and out the door to the backyard. I crawl through the fence, extra careful to avoid getting snagged on the barbwire.

I run like a deer, leaping through the tall grass. At the creek, I look for Little People paddling their leaf boats. I squint my eyes extra narrow so that I can see far up the mountain. But I can't see him. All I see is pine trees. The day goes on forever and when Mr. Brown finally comes down the mountain and crosses the hayfield, his Syílx skin is extra brown from the sun. After dinner, he falls asleep in front of the television with his feet crossed just like Grandpa does.

ċəlċále

"we're going camping today. the huckleberries are ready!"
"Mom, how do you say huckleberries in our language?"
"ċəlċále," the sounds roll off her tongue.
careful to mimic every sound i say, "tsal-tsal-ah."

of all the berries we harvest through the year,
ċəlċále are my favourite.
they are super sweet and tangy, dark purple and super shiny,
with a tiny circle where the stem grasps the berry.

we pack: dishes, pots, cutlery, buckets for picking, sleeping bags,
foamies, a tent, coolers of food, flip-flops, running shoes,
swimsuits, berry-picking clothes, just-in-case-it-rains clothes,
a BBQ, a cowbell, a first-aid kit, and mosquito repellent into the car.

scmém'iʔt sounds like "s-cha-mem-eet."   children
a clan of brown-haired, long and lean children,
we make a bed of blankets in the box of Grandpa's truck.

bounce, bounce, rattle, rattle!
chug, lurch, pop!

a family caravan of cars and trucks
follows Grandpa's old truck
we travel from valley bottom to mountaintop
in search of the perfect huckleberry patch.

seytknmx sounds like "shayt-kin-mux."
the people, the original people are ready
for our annual harvest in the high mountains
all across Interior Salish territory.

a long time ago our Grandmothers and Grandfathers
journeyed by horse and wagon
before that by travois and on moccasin-covered foot
to the highest, most sacred places within our mountains.

trucks, lawn chairs, and tents line the road.
alpine air tingles our noses.
we are here to visit the clouds.
wík'ne ł súsəkʷlíʔ, wík'ne ł súsəkʷlíʔ.   the sacred sees us
sounds like, "week na lh shee-shoo-klee."
we see the sacred in everything and the sacred sees us.
in the mountains, this is what the birds sing all day long.

jingle, jangle, jingle, jangle!

Mom carries a cowbell everywhere we go.
in case of emergency and
to scare our competition away.
birds, called spzúz'uʔ, "sh-peh-zoo-zoo" and   birds
bears, called spéʔec, "sh-pah-atch."   bears

yéyeʔ voices orate childhood memories   grandmother
their voices dance across humid alpine air
buckets tied around their waists; they tie ours too.
"it's important to have two hands free to gather berries
and slap the mosquitoes away."

in town our yéyeʔs need help crossing the road,
but in the berry patch,
sure-footed and stubborn
they are like mountain goats.

climbing over logs
they perch on rocky slopes
in search of ċəlċále bushes
with the fattest berries.

ting, ting, ting

the ċəlċále sing as they fall into our buckets.
like two-handed lightning bolts, we pick berries fast,
eating six, saving two, eating four, saving three.

"don't eat the ċəlċále in your bucket!" my auntie says.
tart, tangy and sweet, we can't resist and stuff handfuls of berries
into our mouths every time their backs are turned.

alpine mountains

"you
girls
have
ċəlċále
all
over
your
faces,"
my
auntie
laughs.
surprised, we look at one another.
dark purple ċəlċále paints our cheeks, lips, and hands.
"cuzzin is purpler!" i say pointing at her. "No you are!" she points
back at me. Suzie is laughing at us but she hasn't seen herself. "let's
have a competition!" "we each have to eat fifty ċəlċále at once then see who's
purplest!" pebbles and rocks fly as we scramble up the mountainside back
to our ċəlċále patch. lightning fast we gather fifty of the fattest berries. "ready!"
Suzie and i holler. "me too!" cuzzin cups her berries to her mouth. Suzie & i copy
her. all of a sudden she screams, "GET READY! GET SET! GO!" we each stuff fifty ċəlċále
berries into our open mouths & then chew extra fast. sweet tangy juice drips down
our chins. "stick out your tongues!" says Grandpa then he inspects our faces because
he is the judge. "you're all purple!" he says. "no one loses and everyone wins." with
sticky hands and tummies full of berries we race to the creek and take turns diving
in. clear blue ice cold glacier water encircles us as we play tag and swim the day
away catching frogs and tadpoles when the sun disappears into alpine mountains
the sky is the color of flames. everyone returns to camp. "you kids gather kindling
for the fire." our moms and aunties all work together making dinner as us kids
gather firewood. when the fire is ablaze we roast marshmallows and hotdogs.
everyone is storytelling about their adventures and who found the biggest
berries. our languages: nɬeʔkepmxcín, nsyílxcn, and english surround
us as we play. in the morning we wake before the birds and sing
wík'ne ɬ súsəkʷlíʔ! wík'ne ɬ súsəkʷlíʔ! we see the sacred in
everything and the sacred sees us. we are ready
to gather ċəlċále all over again.

frog whisperers

Water
crystal
clear
over
rocks
and
stones.
nothing else exists besides
the creek, the mountain, frogs and tadpoles.
glacier cold on ice cube toes purple lips, purple nose. Mom says, "leave those
"wash your purple cheeks!" berry bucket full: stones, sticks, sand, and water.
mucus soft green frog eggs sway in the stream. tadpoles swim mid-transformation.
us girls wait by the smallest eddy in the creek. STONES must be islands for baby tadpoles
growing little web feet swimming fast all alone. us girls want to bring our baby frogs home
even though Mom says, "STOP!" us girls catch baby frogs anyway. we build their
berry bucket home. "put them frogs back in the creek!" "we love frogs!" we say.
"Grandpa." "yes, Sweetheart," he answers.   "how do you say frog?"
"pəpéyɬe," he answers.   "Grandpa,
"Grandpa   i will   will i
don't   never   nor   eat
you   eat   knees   a
think   frog's   frog's
frogs are   webbed
Amazing   Toes

Home
a
frogs
"but   our
says, Auntie   build
cuzzin,   we   to
alone!"   want
frogs

— 37 —

cousin cluster

we are sʔéʔeʔ in Grandpa's garden,   crows
sʔéʔeʔ! sʔéʔeʔ!
child crows we sing, play, and eat everything.

strawberry and raspberry stems,
pea pods and carrot tops mark our steps
and every so often our moms chase us out.

in Grandpa's barn, sun shines between the wooden slats.
we play tag in fragrant hay, climb up and down the ladder
and swing on a braided rope out the loft window.
sometimes we talk amongst ourselves.

Grandpa's blue house has a blue kitchen,
a wood stove in the middle,
a black phone mounted on the wall.
his iron bed is in the living room.
he watches TV with his feet crossed.

Mom has her back to us because she's cooking
macaroni and tomatoes.

"Mom, where did you go to school?"

"st. george's indian residential school.
it was an anglican boarding school.
we had to live there."

"when did you go, Auntie?"
"my bro went first, then your mom, then me.
i was about six years old."

Suzie and i look at cuzzin.
she is the youngest of us three.
"you went by cattle truck when you were a kid,
right Grandpa?"

"yes, that's right."

"Mom, after you went to st. george's,
what did the rest of our aunties and uncles do?"

"foster care took all six of our younger brothers and sisters."

but why?

Métis

Saskatchewan

we arrive by rusted, silver rabbit,
find a log cabin in the snow.
golden orange flames lick kindling
and logs inside a small wood stove.

bear skin, photographs,
Mooshoom's red and black soft plaid
and a child's red vinyl jacket
hang from a hook on the wall.

battered northern pike in a cast iron pan,
Mooshoom stories,
Mooshoom memories.

outside we are illuminated
moonlight and electric reflections
yellow, orange, red, green, blue,
indigo dances across snow.

i wonder how it would feel to stand
in the presence of my father.

i know i would feel safe.
i know i would feel loved.

i gaze into Mooshoom's eyes,
and search for him there.

La Ronge

freshly cut pine and engine oil,
workboots by the door, logging truck outside.
Uncle lights up as he reminisces about
brotherhood adventures.

prairie grass and woodland
sweet strawberry red bubbles in the pot.
hands white with flour, lard and baking powder,
sweet red on fresh oven bread is Auntie's treat

there are no mountains here.
no stones, no clay terraces, no sagebrush.
tall grass and bulrushes line the waterways.

Saskatchewan breeze,
unlike any other kind of breeze.
parched, we swim in a clear blue swimming hole.
our freshwater escape from dust, black flies
and no-see-ums.

homeward we walk, barefoot in soft sand,
bodies a canvas of itchy red welts,
bigger than the palm of my hand.

nighttime echoes as wolves howl
through the jack pines

Mooshoom

curled into
a soft place,
all warm.

i wake
up from under
wool blankets,
patchwork quilts.

in darkness
with each wave
Mooshoom cries
on the shore.

Lac La Ronge
did not take my father.

Mooshoom's sorrow
crashes on the beach
anyway.

i want to go home.
i want my patchwork quilts
within the rising mountains.
no more northern lights.

next morning
at water's edge,
white water froths across stone.

work pants on
jet-black hair
his eyes are brilliant
blue like a Saskatchewan sky.

he casts his rod and reels it in.
an ordinary day
after an ordinary night,
fishing for northern pike.

Back to Batoche, 1985

grass golden, reeds brown,
fiddles sing as feet don't touch the ground,
Métis sash aflame

dancing for 100 years of memories
of Louis Riel and Gabriel Dumont
pay homage to the rights and love of
the people and the land.

somewhere nearby
in the Saskatchewan River
my dad died.

the questions within me always ask
which grassy hill? which turn in the river?
was there gravel or dirt or sand on the beach?

i want to go to that shore
kneel by the water,
wash my tears and pray.

instead i watch aurora borealis through the windshield
curl into warm blankets, listen
while voices, laughter, and people pass by.

Nłeʔkepmxcín
Lullaby

skíxzeʔ transforms

between rage and grief
her child, i watch
my skíxzeʔ,   mother
grasping morning mist.

scáqʷm, zəlkʷúʔ, and sḵepy̓éłp   saskatoon berries,
                                        chokecherries, wild rose bush
sun rises, daylight extends into evening
revolutions around the moon.

green buds push outward,
spring tender, delicate petals
unfold and nourish
hummingbirds and bumblebees.

her mlámn is her stinging bitter thorns   medicine
protection against intrusion
roots woven into land
berries sweet, round, swollen.

scáqʷm bushes, cottonwood, red willow, fir   saskatoon berries
tree families stand united
through winds, rain, and snow.

autumn berry husks and berry bush skeletons
persevere, through the long bitter of winter
broken, battered, bruised.

when springtime returns
the plants on the land
renew themselves.

her oldest child.
i pay witness
as skíxzeʔ transforms

Cəceʔ and Sínciʔ

"Isn't he cold? Why don't they cover him?" My baby brother has yellow jaundice. My mom said to call him "sínciʔ" because that means younger brother. He's asleep under the blue lights of the incubator. His feet and arms are curled inward because his body is still unfolding from living inside my mom's tummy. I stand on salt and pepper linoleum, nose to the glass, twelve years old. May 1, 1985. My sínciʔ was born on our auntie's birthday. "The best birthday present ever," that is what she said. And he was born by caesarean, just like my baby sister—my mom always tells me to call her "cəceʔ." Cəceʔ is pronounced cha-cha, and sínciʔ is pronounced shin-chee.

"I'm sure it's warm in there." Auntie responds. "They wouldn't let baby catch a chill. Did you guys name him yet?"

My mom moves slowly in her pink hospital gown, robe, and slippers. She's pushing a little cart with her iv.

"Mike Junior," she responds.

"Awww, Mike Junior. That's a perfect name!" Auntie answers.

Eight pounds, eleven ounces at birth, my sínciʔ has beautiful, black huckleberry eyes just like my cəceʔ. There's a tiny bit of disappointment inside me. I didn't get to name my sínciʔ as I did my cəceʔ. I suppose being named after his dad is a good thing. I do not understand yellow jaundice as the only thing yellow about him is his tiny nightshirt. He has perfect brown skin, perfect feet, perfect fingers, tiny arms, and a perfect chest just like my cəceʔ. Soon, the heavy door whooshes open and the nurse, wearing soft white running shoes, walks in. She helps my mom back into bed, then checks her iv. She checks on us too, making sure there aren't too many of us in the room. "Immediate family only!" We always agree. Of course, only our immediate family will visit my mom and newborn brother. One thing I know about hospitals is the nurses always get upset when even a little bit of our family comes to visit. The hospital room is too small and my aunties laugh too loud for the nurses' comfort.

When Mom changes my sínciʔ's diaper, his lower back is an array of purple, blue, and green. It looks as though he has bruises. If it were the sky, it would be the northern lights. "Look! My sínciʔ has a birthmark on his bum too, just like my cəceʔ." I inspect the mark as my mom changes his diaper. I'm still not allowed to touch him because of the yellow jaundice.

"All Native babies have them at birth," Auntie answers. "Non-Native babies don't have them." Instantly a hundred thoughts fly into my mind.

"Really? Why do only Native babies have them?" I pause for a moment before asking my next question. "It looks like a bruise though. Did the doctor spank him? A kid at school said they spank newborn babies to make them breathe." Why would anyone do that to a baby?

"Actually, it's not a birthmark. And no, doctors don't spank babies. That's not true." It was the nurse answering this time. "Oh? Gee that's good." I breathe a sigh of relief because ever since I heard that, I was really worried they had done that to my sínciʔ and my cəceʔ too.

"It's actually called a Mongolian mark," the nurse continued.

"Hmmm. Why are they called 'Mongolian' if only Native babies have them?" I'd seen this nurse before, when my mom had my cəceʔ. "Is Mongolia a country?"

"Yes, it is a country in Asia."

"The mark disappears as baby grows older. That's why you can't see yours anymore." I turn and look at my auntie in shock.

"Really? I had one?" That's when my sínciʔ starts crying, toes wide in a newborn wail. The nurse picks him up and carefully passes him to my mom. My mom adjusts her top and my brother starts nursing immediately, his tiny cheeks intent as he looks into her eyes. His arms and legs are so skinny in comparison to his itty-bitty potbelly.

Day after day Mom soaks, washes, and bleaches cloth diapers. My sínciʔ received a cradleboard and babybasket too, just like my cəceʔ. They are traditional Nłeʔkepmx baby beds, except his is made with blue fabric and buckskin ties down the front. The cradleboard is secured onto a long, oval-shaped piece of wood that is about six inches longer than the length of his body. This is to allow space for him to grow. At first when my brother is wrapped and tied, he's mad, but as time passes, the cradleboard becomes his favourite place to sleep.

One day Mr. Brown, my stepdad, takes my sínciʔ, sleeping soundly and laced tightly in his cradleboard, and hangs his board from a hook on the wall. My sínciʔ continues sleeping for a while and when he wakes, he doesn't even cry. He just observes his surroundings in silence like a painting on the wall.

"Michael Brown, where is my son?" Mom's voice is higher than normal as she searches for my sínciʔ. Moments later she is standing in front of his cradleboard with his dad close by, smiling. My sínciʔ had already been watching her even though it took her a few seconds to find him. The gentle warmth of Mr. Brown's laughter fills our house.

Chubby and shiny like miniature Buddhas, both my cɔceʔ and sínciʔ love sucking their baby cloths while bathing in the kitchen sink or a plastic baby tub on the kitchen table. And when they grow too big for that, they bathe together in the big bathtub. They splash water everywhere. Afterwards, they are fresh with baby lotion, clean cotton diapers, crinkly plastic pants, and soft, one-piece pajamas.

Two of everything: two chubby sets of hands, two sets of chubby brown feet, two high chairs, two sets of baby dishes, two pairs of shoes, two one-piece snowsuits, two sets of mittens, two scarves, and one big diaper bag. My cɔceʔ was already running when Sínciʔ wobbled his first steps from one person to the next, chair to chair, in high-top booties. From breast milk to "ba-bas," first word, first bite of solid food, little jars of mashed carrots, mashed potatoes, mashed pears, and baby spoons. Sticky apple juice and spaghetti sauce smeared all over their hair, faces, high chairs, and floor.

Asleep in their crib, sometimes I can't tell if they are breathing. Standing at the bedroom door, I sneak quiet steps forward and peer through the crib bars, anxiously watching and waiting for their chests to rise and fall. Sometimes I put my hand on their tiny chests, waiting for their next breath. Mom is always whispering loudly for me to leave them alone when they sleep. "Don't you wake my babies!" Moments later, the babies wake one another anyway and start shaking the sides of the crib, spinning rattles and calling out in baby talk. And of course, Mom hollers at me for waking them again.

Owies and Band-Aids with pictures. A big fall and a bonk on Sínciʔ's forehead leaves a goose egg that does not go away. Mom has carefully planned family photos on our front lawn. We all pose, and that goose egg is the main highlight every time we look at the photos.

Baby smiles grow into big, drooly grins and baby teeth: Orajel, gripe water, Baby Aspirin and then baby's first words, first sentences, and first questions. "Sister? Sister, wazzat? Why? Sister, why?"

Baby moccasins and tiny, thumb-sized baby socks grow to little girl socks with ribbons and pink tights, little boy socks with stripes, sailor suits and bow ties, frilly dresses and buckle-up shoes. Fast running shoes for a super fast little boy. Backward shoes, grass stains, bugs, hugs, snuggles, bedtime stories, and kisses. Teasing and fights at the kitchen table. "Who wants cheese to go with their whine?" When I am in the bathroom doing my thing, they cry at the door, "Pee, Sisterrrr! PEE!!" Positive that my cɔceʔ is fibbing I refuse to open the door.

"Open the door! Your cɔceʔ needs to go pee!" Mom bangs on the bathroom door and hollers. Little people with purpose they march in: chubby cheeks, chubby legs, bare feet, and potty training underpants, "Doing, Sister? Doing?"

"Ga?" Our sínciʔ toddles along, following my cɔceʔ's every step.

"MOM! I TOLD YOU!" My footsteps stomping away often hurt their feelings. I always have to turn back and reassure them, even when I don't want to.

Rockstar Hair

"Mom, can I go to the movies tonight?" It's my first New Year's Eve as a teenager. I want to do something fun. I want to go dancing with my friends.

"A movie? There isn't a movie on New Year's Eve." She raises her eyebrows at me. Think fast, think fast! I struggle to keep a straight face. "Your aunties and uncles, everyone's coming over. You should stay home."

"I don't want to stay home though. I want to go to the movies with my friends. I'm positive there's one showing tonight. It's a special New Year's Eve movie."

"Hmm." She's counting stitches on her knitting. "Well, I want you to call the theatre and make sure."

"Okay." I've broken into an instant sweat. My face is hot. I grab the phone book and flip through the Yellow Pages, searching for the movie theatre.

The answering machine picks up quickly with the recording, "Happy Holidays! This is the Merritt Theatre. We are closed the following dates through the Christmas holidays: December 24th, 25th, 26th and December 31st and January 1st."

"Hello? Oh hi, I was just wondering which movie was playing tonight for New Year's Eve." I pause as though listening to their response. "Oh, okay, thank you!" I'm shaking inside with my lies. "Mom, I'm going to the nine o'clock movie with Wendy."

"With who?" Wendy is a new friend. She's in grade nine so she's a bit older.

"Wendy, um, Joseph, from Shulus. I think her mom's name is Harriet. You know her mom." She calms down when she realizes who I'm talking about.

"What time will the movie finish?"

"I think at about eleven." She wants to move again, this time to Vancouver so she can finish her teaching degree at The University of British Columbia. She's talking about finishing it now that my baby brother and baby sister are a little bit older. She said that in order for her to complete her teaching degree, we have to move to UBC, and the babies have to go to daycare on campus. She has even put in her application for family housing. I don't want to move to Vancouver. I want to stay with my friends.

"Hmm…" She's still knitting and seems disappointed, but she doesn't say no.

My mind is racing as I dash to my room and turn on my curling iron. I am a student in my older cousin's academy, "Teenager 101: How to Be Cool." Long hours of mentoring include watching her choose her clothes, fix her hair, and apply her makeup. As a result, all of us need to have spiral perms, just like her, and wear tight pants, just like her. And now, I have rockstar hair, feathered all the way back, just like her.

How to Have Perfectly Feathered Hair:
1) Preheat curling iron and blow-dry hair.
2) For thick Indian hair one must apply the first coat of Finesse Extra Hold Hairspray while hair is in the preheated curling iron. Do not feather until all hair is completely curled.
3) Feather with a special brush, backcomb, add additional curls as needed.

4) Hairspray again, backcomb some more until perfection is achieved.
5) Apply more Finesse Extra Hold Hairspray. Upon completion the hair should be perfectly solid.

I quickly search my drawer for my tightest jeans and best T-shirt. It's a good thing I've been under my sister-cuzzin's mentorship. Otherwise I wouldn't have a clue what to wear. But she showed me another trick and it works like a charm.

How to Put on Super-Tight Jeans:
1) Insert first leg and then second leg.
2) Jump up and down until they're up.
3) Suck in your tummy.
4) If that doesn't work, lay on the bed.
5) If that doesn't work, get a friend to help.
Note: Cinch the top button closed first. Then do up the zipper.

Wendy said they were on their way. When they toot their horn, I grab my jean jacket and run for the door. "Okay, see you later, Mom! Happy New Year's!"

"Come here, I want to look at you."

Oh no! Now what? I stop dead in my tracks and then turn around and trudge back to the top of the stairs.

"How are you getting home?" She stops knitting and looks at me. My stomach turns over. I internally review all the disciplinary actions she might take when she figures out where I've really gone.

"I'll catch a ride home with Wendy." My face is numb with my lie. I hope she can't tell by my expression.

"What time will you be home?" This is it. My first time lying about my real destination. I'm going out.

"After the movie ends, I think around eleven-thirty." She nods her head and goes back to her knitting. I run for the front door before she can ask more questions.

Once the winter air is on my face and the gate is swinging closed, I'm free. It's my first dance at Spaxomin Rez and I'm super-duper excited. Wendy and I are abuzz during the hour-long drive. Her sister is driving, and the music is turned up loud all the way there.

Spaxomin Hall is electric with fancy lights and a DJ. This is the same place where they had my mom's wedding reception. The only other dances I've gone to are the grade eight Halloween and Christmas dances at our high school, and my elementary school dances.

The lights are low, and everyone is standing with their backs to the walls or sitting at tables. There aren't many people, but Wendy's sister says it's still early. We manage to swindle a two-litre bottle of Tropikiwi cooler from somewhere. We go outside and take turns drinking from the bottle. It tastes foul, like cough medicine, but we're cool so we drink it anyway. People are standing around, walking to their cars, going in and out the doors.

The DJ is playing a mixture of country, old school, and top hits music. It is 1987 and I'm electric underneath the flashing lights. My legs going this way, arms going that way. I have the dancing groove. That's when I see him across the room. He's wearing a cowboy hat, cowboy boots, and Wrangler jeans, and to Creedence Clearwater Revival, he's a dancing machine. If this is the beginning of teenage-hood, this really could be fun.

K̓ece? Tea

Uncle's truck is a slow-moving tank as it pulls out of the yard onto Dodding Avenue. The wooden cow box is loaded with furniture and boxes as high as the truck roof. We are headed for the Coquihalla Highway on our way to Vancouver. This is only the second time I've ever travelled to Vancouver. We are moving into family housing on campus at the University of British Columbia, except my mom calls it UBC. Mom needs two more years of university to finish her teaching degree. After that she will be a schoolteacher. My cəce?, my sínci?, my oldest cousin, and I are all moving to the city with her. I'm happy my cousin is moving in with us. Mom's oldest sister's oldest daughter. We've spent so much time together since I was little, she is more of a big sister. She wants to finish grade twelve in Vancouver.

Our dog Max is sitting by the columbine, watching the truck as we drive away. My stepdad gathered seeds from the columbine wildflowers when we were huckleberry picking up the Coquihalla Mountains. He brought them home and planted the seeds beside our front door. Columbine are so much prettier than the dark-green, jagged-tipped plants he has growing in our backyard. Columbine have a wide range in colour from flaming yellowish orange-red to bluish purple when they are in full bloom. The actual flower looks like a cluster of blossom hummingbirds. Each delicate petal unfolding is like the opening of wings. I love wildflowers. Indian paintbrush, fireweed, lady slippers, sunflowers, wild roses, chocolate lilies, tiger lilies, and water lilies to name only a few. In my childhood dreams the chocolate lily roots taste like chocolate almonds and the petals are chocolate too and little people wear the lady slippers. In my childhood dreams, the little people visit every single wildflower because the mountains are their sacred, perfectly manicured gardens. Wildflowers from the highest mountains are the most beautiful gift because you have to travel far to find them.

My stepdad knows the name of every kind of plant, flower, bush, tree, and all their relatives too. I didn't even know plants had relatives and latin names. Ever since he started the Nicola Valley Institute of Technology forestry program he has been collecting all kinds of books. Now everywhere we go, he's saying the names of things. He not only knows the latin and the english plant names; he knows a few of the Nsyílxcn and Nłeʔkepmxcín names as well. My auntie knows the names of hundreds of plants in our language but not all the english names. She knows all the steps for harvesting and processing hundreds of plants. She has magic hands and can weave and spin so quickly that if you blink, you will miss how she did it. Auntie grew up with her grandmother because she didn't go to Indian Residential School. She has knowledge of our plants and medicines because the priests and nuns didn't scrub away her memories.

One thing I have learned is how plants can change from one season to the next. What is edible in the spring is not always edible in the summer and its use can change because the medicinal properties can intensify as the seasons change. For example, stinging nettle. The newborn shoots can be steamed and eaten early in the spring. Later in the season, the plant and its parts (roots, leaves, etc.) can be carefully harvested for use as a tea or bath, or topically as a rub. The other thing I have learned is that many plants have what I consider a twin. Often, the twin will look similar, but with variations in appearance such as different coloured blossoms or leaves. More importantly, the twin is often toxic or can even be deathly poisonous. For example, nodding onion looks almost identical to death camas and they can grow side-by-side in the same terrain. So similar in fact, I don't feel comfortable even talking about how to identify the differences.

Labrador tea, trapper's tea, or swamp tea in the english language is an example that I do feel comfortable talking about. In my language we call this tea, ḱéceʔ. As far as I know, it grows across Canada. In the Nicola Valley, there are two kinds of Labrador tea that we drink: One kind is shiny under the leaves and the second kind has rust-coloured fuzz on the underside. When you harvest it, you need to be careful not to accidentally gather bog laurel. Bog laurel is also called "swamp laurel" and it is considered poisonous; however, it apparently has medicinal uses that I have never been taught. Bog laurel is a smaller plant and its leaves are similar in appearance to Labrador tea. However, bog laurel grows pink blossoms in the springtime and Labrador tea has white blossoms. The blossoms generally fall off by summer. The most important recognizable year-round feature is the underside of bog laurel leaves have a distinctly white fuzz. Bog laurel grows in the same type of marshy or mountainous landscapes as our ḱéceʔ tea. I've heard people say that our ḱéceʔ tea, with the shiny under-leaves, also contains traces of toxic alkaloids and an oil called ledum that is apparently considered toxic for humans.

The most common and recommended species, based on my observations, seems to be the plant with rust-coloured fuzz on the underside of the leaves. I've been told numerous ways to harvest and brew ḱéceʔ tea by my Elders and aunties and yes, it can be quite confusing.

How to Harvest Ḱéce? Tea

1) Only harvest the plant with the rust-coloured fuzz on the underside of the leaves.
2) We've only ever used the Labrador tea with shiny dark-green leaves; now we are told not to use them.
3) You should never boil ḱéce? tea.
4) Boiling ḱéce? tea kills the alkaloids. (Is that even possible?)
5) I grew up always boiling our shiny-leaved ḱéce? tea. And finally,
6) ONLY steep ḱéce? tea and NEVER boil it.

People swear by every method. To be honest, since I was a kid, we have always boiled our ḱéce?. When it was too strong, we added more water. When it was too weak, we added more leaves. I always felt relaxed afterwards, especially if I had an upset tummy. Even so, because of this uncertainty, it is probably safest to steep Labrador tea and not boil it. Even though I always boil it and never steep it. Yes, this information is very confusing.

When we were kids, we would pile blankets in the box of the truck and ride in the back. We would lay in the back with the wind whistling over our heads along the dirt roads all the way up to the Coquihalla Mountains. It always felt like the drive took forever. Nowadays, the Coquihalla Highway is a huge, gaping maw of black pavement and bright white lines that travels right through our traditional berry-picking grounds. The cliff faces along the highway are freshly cut and surrounded by jagged stones. The Nicola Valley is a bowl between the mountains: full of family and memories.

Mom used to ride her orange ten-speed bike with me in the basket seat all the way to town. The dirt and pavement were all a blur when I looked at the ground. We'd ride through Shulus Reserve and sometimes visit Auntie. Sometimes, we would stop to visit at Grandpa's house on our way to town. I wonder if I drove her crazy the way my brother and sister drive me crazy? I must've been heavy. She must've been strong. I've wiped out so many times on my bike. I wonder if she ever wiped out on hers?

Legs and arms stretched way out, my banana seat bike was my Harley-Davidson. One time I hit a bump and backflipped right on the street by my house. My neighbour's mom was standing in her yard. She came running. "Oh my goodness, are you okay?" she asked, but she couldn't stop laughing and I was crying with scrapes on both knees and elbows too. "I'm so sorry!" she said wiping tears, "but that had to be the funniest thing I ever saw."

Everyone from elementary school went their separate ways when we reached grade eight. Instead of classmates and friends, everyone became white preppies, jocks and cowboys, Natives and preppy Natives, nerds and geeks, head bangers and smokers. The in-crowd and the out-crowd. Then there were the couples, steady girlfriends and boyfriends. And what if you didn't have the right clothes? And then there were the fist fights. I don't know how to fight. When Arlene Jasper caught me, yet again on the school steps, my punches were a crazy flail for self-protection that I think ended up connecting with her, somewhere? We went to elementary school together but in high school I became a target, hunted. All I ever wanted was to be her friend, but I never was. All I wanted was to fit in, but I didn't. I was Indian; she was white.

Maybe I brought everything on myself. I can't help reliving those moments even though I am trying so hard to forget them. I am trying hard not to think about it.

Last month—or was it two months ago it happened?—I was stranded in town and missed the school bus. He offered me a ride. When we arrived at my house, I was surprised when he asked to come inside. He walked around our empty house; my mom was at school and my stepdad at work. Then he grabbed me and kissed me hard, with sloppy huge lips. He slobbered all over my cheeks and chin. I didn't know how to kiss like that. Then he pushed and pulled me into my mom's bedroom. I told him no, but he wouldn't listen to me.

For an instant, I thought maybe he had fallen in love with me, but that thought quickly passed. He didn't care. I should have kicked and fought him, but he was hockey-player strong. "No." I said, "Stop. Let me go. I'm not ready for this." I tried pulling away, but he wouldn't let me go. He wouldn't stop. When he pulled off my pants, pain, confusion, and shame filled ceiling and walls. "No! Please stop."

The same hurt and confusion that had overwhelmed me at eleven...when the one man I wanted to believe in betrayed me. Betrayed my child body with his drunk, groping hands. Then yet again, by a friend's groping father. Violated. Afraid. Self-hate flowed into my arms, legs, toes, tips of hair. Trust no one. Never trust. Confused about the roles of men. Hurt. I hoped he would apologize; say he was sorry, that what he did was wrong. That stealing someone's virginity was wrong. Instead, everywhere I go, I am hunted. What is worse? What he did, or the actions of the women in denial? They hate me in order to protect him. From what, himself? What is wrong with protecting me? For standing up for me? I am scared to walk down the street. They always find me when I'm alone. I am always alone. If I had a big brother or a dad, would my dad protect me? Why did this happen? What did I do wrong? Do girls ever lose their virginity to someone who loves them?

I always wanted a dad. I always wanted a big brother. I wanted love and protection. I wrongly believed he would treat me like a little sister. I wanted to be a younger sister to a big, strong older brother. I thought older brothers were warriors for their sisters. At high school, there are always couples standing around in the hallways at school. When I was in elementary school, back in grade six and seven, there were one or two boyfriend-girlfriend couples even though we were all still children. I remember feeling uncertain, wondering how it worked, to have a boyfriend when we were still children in elementary school. Back then and even now, I wonder what it felt like to be loved and to feel safe.

As we leave the valley and travel west on the highway, Merritt becomes smaller and smaller in the distance and all my fears and worries change. We're moving towards something new and I'm afraid. I'm glad we're leaving. I never want to return, and yet part of me doesn't want to go. The Nicola Valley is the home of my ancestors. These mountains are my home.

The closer we get to the city, the busier the highway becomes, until the highway is stop-and-go, rush-hour traffic. We've been following Mom's car. Highway 1 exits onto Grandview Highway, and we continue travelling west past rows of rundown houses until Grandview turns into 12th Avenue. The Vancouver General Hospital is the biggest hospital I've ever seen. On West 10th Avenue the streets are lined with perfect heritage houses with perfect lawns and cathedral-tall trees. The University of British Columbia is straight across the city above the Pacific Ocean.

My cousin and I registered at Kitsilano Secondary School. Kitsilano is three stories tall, huge compared to Merritt Secondary School. It's only the very beginning of September, and my cousin is busy collecting wedding magazines because she wants a beautiful lace grad dress. She also wants to go to college after she graduates, so she is researching post-secondary programs in Vancouver. Suzie makes two friends; one is italian, and one is greek. They are both stunningly beautiful and funny. She gets a part-time job for evenings after school at an ice cream store right beside Kitsilano Beach. She brings home different kinds of ice cream all the time. My favourite ice cream is "Pralines and Cream," and her favourite is "World Class Chocolate." I submit my first-ever resume to Baskin-Robbins, but they won't hire me. Yet.

"Fourteen years old is too young," they said. "Come back when you're fifteen." Time passes so slowly when Suzie leaves for her shift. I hang around her work and help her at closing time: wash windows, sweep and mop the floor, wipe counters. I'm just not allowed behind the counter. I submit my resume again and again. On my fifteenth birthday, in November, Baskin-Robbins finally hires me.

On days off, we take the Downtown bus to Granville Street and go shopping at Pacific Centre Mall. The best part about the city is the non-stop music on the radio, shopping malls, and the beach. But the feelings of loneliness don't go away. We sneak into nightclubs and dance until the bar closes. I want to walk down my own street, in my own neighbourhood, and hear the dogs bark. I want to wake up to the fresh morning scent of our mountains.

Mom and I don't laugh together, we argue. She's under a lot of stress with all of us, and I'm not making it any easier on her. When I tell her what happened, she turns her back on me. Shame. Is it my fault? Is it fear? Is this how we're programmed to be? Everything is my fault. Everything. Too many long-distance phone calls, too much attitude. What do moms and daughters talk about anyway? I don't care about anything anymore. Vancouver partying takes on a life of its own until this fifteen-year-old gets kicked out.

University of British Columbia

cement humid cityscape chokes the breath
we navigate an enormous grid
pavement, houses, buildings, vehicles
until cement disappears

everything turns to salad
fiddlehead ferns, stinky skunk cabbage
busy roads disappear into greenery

vibrant and luminescent
when the university emerges.
i am awed by a different kind of hush.

we roll past official buildings,
the university bookstore and people
walking with backpacks and school texts.

the city contrasts against everything familiar
arid sparse semi-desert landscape and dry dusty wind
cottonwood, red willow bushes, wild roses, pine trees.

this is a university
where are the Natives?

Blackout

The house in Lower Nicola is empty without family. Black 35-mm film containers, packs of cigarette papers, matches, and a twirling vine plant sit on the shelf across the kitchen window. We have skin and bones for furniture. The fridge has all my favourites: eggs, ketchup, Cheez Whiz, and bologna with my McCain Hashbrowns in the freezer. Macaroni with Cheez Whiz is my second favourite meal; hashbrowns mixed with scrambled eggs, bacon, and ketchup is my number one.

When they're home, our house comes alive. But when they're gone, it's empty, lonely, and silent. They are always gone. So it's always empty, lonely, and silent. At least when Mom was doing the Native Indian Teacher Education Program (NITEP) in Kamloops, before the babies were born, we always came home on weekends, but Vancouver is too far. Now, there isn't even enough junk lying around to have a messy house. The dust gathers just the same.

My stepdad is rarely home. Or maybe it's me who's rarely home. He's always going out the back door to smoke and he's started drinking too, although not in our house. Then he's quiet. He's really, really quiet. He's just a quiet-natured person but that means we rarely talk. Do dads talk to their daughters? What do dads talk about? Maybe he just doesn't know how to talk to me either. Girls with dads must feel safe. Girls with dads must feel loved. I don't have to sneak out of our house anymore. Now when I want to go to a bush party, I just walk out the front door. Fifteen, mouthy, defiant, kicked out of home, school, and Vancouver. I drink any time, all the time: Kokanee, Budweiser, hard stuff but too paranoid to toke. My stepdad's greenery remains on the shelf. I skip out or show up for school whenever I want. Anything goes because I'm alone.

My childhood best friend. I stand by her when she's broken. My only golden friend, my childhood everything. I gather her pieces and put her back together again. Small town judgment and gossip take a new twist. slut. drunk. drug user. thief. Indian. She doesn't want to be your friend. Too brown. Too white. Too damn real for you. Inside, hurt is twisted into shame. Tired from days and nights of trying to fit in. The weekend partying becomes weekdays. The passed-out drunk girl wakes to the theft of body, spirit. I don't give a fuck. I just keep getting drunk.

Carrot sticks, homemade appys, music up loud—it's late afternoon when an onslaught of partygoers appears. Ice cubes in tall glasses of Long Island Iced Tea is the mix. We drink and eat carrot sticks until sunlight recedes and darkness sets in. When the mix runs dry, it's Kokanee beer. It's rye and coke, vodka and orange juice, or Tropikiwi wine coolers again. Anything goes until these amalgamated brews become carrot soup bile projectile style. Yeehaw it's another blackout on the back steps for this teenage rockstar.

for the party

on the hillside in darkness,
flames crackle and sway
reaching skyward.
silently beckoning for the young
and we gather.

the city is not my home.
alone.
something inside is broken.

pain, confusion, shame
i thought a kiss was okay.
no! stop please. fear.

trapped beneath
weight squeezing
the breath
out. of. me.

Mom's patchwork quilt
squares brown with flecks of blue
tear-reflected images
clear in peripheral view

legs pushed apart in springtime
as snow and ice melted
and sun awakened memories
of huckleberries and swimming.

journal entries on scraps of paper,
skewed thoughts of death,
a random plan.
worthless.

pockets full of change,
walk out the front door,
six-pack hanging off fingertips

drink to have fun.
drink to forget.
drink to fit in.
drink to hide

this fear.
this pain.
this rage.
this shame.

Tmíxʷ—This Land

Sk̓ʷóz has a big garden right where my great-grandparents had theirs. She has their photos on the wall, standing in the garden with their dog and everything growing all around them. Great-Grandpa and Great-Grandma were her mom and dad. My sk̓ʷóz is my grandpa's younger sister. She explained that "sk̓ʷóz" translates as an affectionate term for grand-auntie, or perhaps I add "affectionate" to the translation because I love her so much. She always has stories to tell. She cooks breakfast every morning, toast with eggs sunny-side up. She loves Indian medicines, roots, and Indian tea. She bakes fresh apple pie, and I wake every morning to her Nłeʔkepmxcín lullaby: the tinkle of laughter and gossip, Elder style. She's always smiling. She tells me stories and gives me hugs. She taught me how to make never-fail pastry dough for Grandpa's favourite, apple pie. I live right across the highway from my grandpa's house. When I look out my new bedroom window, I see my uncle's horses kicking up dust in Grandpa's corrals. I can go be a nuisance at Grandpa's house any time I want.

My cousin doesn't know it, but my heart grows in spite of his constant teasing and laughter. He takes me for rides on the back of his motorcycle. I am so terrified all I can do is scream. He teaches me to drive standard transmission. Rolling back and forth on the cattle guard, truck stuttering as we do the chicken, he hollers, "Jesus christ, step on the clutch!" My cousin becomes the big brother I never had. I am annoying. I am his shadow. I just want to follow him everywhere he goes. I want to wear his sweaters, be his bratty little sister, and eat the last piece of apple pie. He drives me to school in the morning and brings me home too. He accepts me on the days when I am a broken, shattered mess. He teaches me to drink shooters and we skip out of school. Head in the toilet, forehead resting on the rim, tears falling into the ceramic bowl. "Nic! Jesus christ, Nic. What's the matter?" On hands and knees, I crawl across the living room floor, puke still on my chin.

"I want to stop drinking. I can't do this anymore. This isn't who I am. This isn't how I want to live. I don't want to grow old like this." If this isn't who I am, then who am I? It's true. I'm done.

"Aww, everything will be okay, you'll see," he says. Then I pass out for the rest of the day.

—

In the sunlight her T-shirt rests across her belly, round like green watermelon flesh on sweet red fruit. Like our cat lying sideways across the middle of the kitchen floor, pink skin exposed, her belly shifts as her unborn baby wiggles inside. She should be resting but she ain't no cat. Today she has a bellyache and she wants to walk. My second youngest auntie is a small lady with a really big laugh.

Her ex was mean. On Quilchena Avenue I look in his eyes, rage overpowering fear. "I don't like you. I want you to stop hurting her. You have to stop!" I dislike him even more because he's friendly when he's sober. Afterwards I am angry with myself. I fear that I made it worse for her and I'm angry for the moments when I like him enough to wish he would just change, but despite his promises to her, he never does.

When I was younger I wasn't allowed to go to my godmom's house if she was drinking. The old A-frame house had a huge driveway, and a big shed filled with tools. The ground inside was black from old engine oil. There was a clothesline that crossed the yard. Tiny, her old lassie dog, always sat on the front step, welcoming everyone who came to visit. One day after school, I caught the school bus into town and walked from my young mom's office to check on my godmom. My goddaddy had moved into his own house. My godmom was sad and alone after that. I found an old-timer I didn't know, sitting at her kitchen table. They were drunk. That old man's sense of self-righteousness was no comparison to the fury of an eleven-year-old. He was no comparison to my worry for her safety and well-being. On the table, I found a tall bottle of alcohol, half full. I checked the cupboards and the fridge and found one more. The long glass necks were cold in my hands. I carried them to the kitchen sink and she came running from the other room, hollering, "Hey! Damn you, Babygirl! Put those back! Those are mine!"

"You have to stop drinking, Mom! You're not allowed to drink anymore, Mom! NO MORE! I HATE IT WHEN YOU DRINK, MOM! I'm not allowed to come here when you're drinking, Mom!" Then I turned to that man and I roared, "GET OUT OF HERE!" Eyes glued on their faces, daring them to come closer. I poured the liquid down the drain and refilled the bottles with cold, clear water, sacred water. She stood in the doorway not moving, because she was Mommy and I was Babygirl.

"Goddamn alcohol. God damn it anyways. I'm never, ever going to drink. Never ever in my whole entire life." I slammed the front door so hard the whole house shook when I left. Then cried all the way back to my young mom's office. "Dammit, damn you, damn everything in the whole damn world! Damn it anyways!" All I wanted to do was to fix her, but she was stubborn too.

Beside you I imagine myself as your protector, Səx^wsúx^w, grizzly bear woman. Fierce and unafraid, I guide you through the darkness into brilliance once again. If only I knew the way. I want something... someone to show me the way.

All day my young auntie and I talk, we tease, we laugh, and we walk because we're good at those things, just like we're good at gathering berries. I am perturbed by her tummy pains so even when she tells me to go, I refuse to leave her. I'm thinking maybe she ate something bad. When we reach the river she says, "Let's keep walking." On the bridge she says, "Let's walk to the hill." At the hill she says, "Let's go to the hospital." If I could carry her I would, but she's too big, so we walk and we talk and we laugh some more.

With each step down that long road, I worry for her, her belly enormous and round. I think of the ancients whose blood runs through our veins. Did they live in peace day to day, as they travelled through this valley? My mom walked this road many times, too. When my aunties and uncles were taken away to foster homes, she was a young girl just out of residential school. She didn't want to lose touch with them. She would walk all the way into town from one house to the other and take them for visits.

Our ancestral Syílx, Nłeʔkepmx, and Athapaskan Grandmothers, pregnant mothers must have walked this path before us. Every realm of the "Nicola" Valley, every one of the ten thousand waterways, carries the shadows of their footsteps. Tmíx^w, temxulax^w—this land—throbs with a cadence and pulse of generations of Indigenous women—mind, body, spirit intertwined with the spirits and life force of the land. A positioning-repositioning journey, walking as their unborn baby turns and shifts, prepares to travel the birth canal. Ancient mothers full of prayers for the tender spirits of their unborn and newly born. My auntie doesn't know it yet, but she is surrounded by the loving embrace of our ancestral Grandmothers.

When we reach the emergency room entrance, the nurses take one long look at my aunt and escort her right in. "She's in labour!" they say. Auntie is worried about me. She thinks I need a barf bag. Arms flailing, she moves on the birthing table as though to get one for me.

"As if!" I say, and she laughs out loud because she is strapped to the birthing table. Her laugh has a pain-filled pitch I've never heard before or since. Moments later, a baby girl comes singing her birthing song, coated in birthing waters. A newborn baby, her tiny voice pierces the white hospital walls. My first thought as I see her newborn perfection is *k*ʷ*məmʼiʔmeʔ pʼéskeʔ.* Tiny and perfect hummingbird. This is my newborn cousin.

Things will get better. She is my strength and I am hers and we pay witness to each other's growth. We struggle sometimes fall but we always get up again. It will take time and endurance, I know it will, but things WILL get better. As I walk down the white marbled floors through the long hospital hallway and exit through the front doors, I make a promise to myself.

I will never drink again.

Grandpa's Corrals

Everything in the world is suddenly awake and growing. The fields are peppered with green. The brilliant shoots are discreet at first; silent and tiny they emerge, bursting through the grey, black, and brown shades of soil, sand, and clay. Saskatoon berry bushes and lilac bushes are blossoming white and fragrant purple, awakening the land with their beauty. If we listen carefully, we can hear the land singing wind songs that never end. They sing their blessings of beauty and strength throughout our entire valley. Scẃéxmxuym̓xʷ, Syílx temxulaxʷ like a weaving we are intertwined/interconnected. As we drink from the ten thousand waterways that irrigate this valley, as we breathe our ancestors' breath and walk in the shadows of our Grandmothers' and Grandfathers' footsteps. Until we return to tmíxʷ and our children walk in the trails we have broken. We know, there is no beginning, no end. We are a part of this spiral that keeps spinning.

Every morning, through my bedroom walls I hear the musical voice of my skʷóz, speaking Nɬeʔkepmxcín on the telephone. If I listen closely, I catch words that I understand and I remember more and more. My skʷóz, my grandpa's younger sister, has been teaching me Nɬeʔkepmxcín every day. Through her kind, gentle love, the great lonely fissures in my heart are healing.

The horses raise clouds of dust as they run circles around Grandpa's corrals. I watch them as I walk on tiptoe along the rotting, wooden cattle guard. Among the many dreams I've had of travelling trails through the mountains, I dreamt of a wagon and horses rolling along a long gravel road. Mountains on either side, it rolled past where my grand-uncle's farm is now, leaving clouds of dust behind. At one time, there was a huge pine tree by the entrance to my sk̫óz's driveway. Over the years, so many vehicles crashed into it, the Department of Highways had it cut down. A huge stump remained, and people continued crashing into that until they finally removed the stump as well. The weird thing was that once the tree was completely removed, no one crashed there anymore.

"Hi Grandpa!" I call as I walk inside. Grandpa has a typical government house: blue exterior and blue interior, a blue front step, a blue kitchen, two blue bedrooms, and a big purple lilac bush right beside his front door. Nothing changes at Grandpa's house. His old iron bed in the living room. His favourite slippers sitting by his bed. They are faded golden, curly-toed East Indian shoes that he got from an "East Indian fella" who didn't have enough cash, back when Grandpa was the town bootlegger. That guy returned to get his shoes when he had money to pay, but Grandpa liked the shoes so much that he kept them. He wore those curly-toed shoes until my uncle claimed them. Then my uncle wore them everywhere, even to the rodeo grounds. Grandpa has a brand-new television with a wireless remote control. But today, he's not watching TV. "Grandpa, are you home?" I holler extra loud.

Grandpa loves taking photographs and his walls are covered in photographs of family, especially from Indian rodeos. When Uncle made it to the Indian National Finals Rodeo for bull riding in Albuquerque, New Mexico, Grandpa bought a fancy 35-mm camera with a special telescope and a fast-action lens. His new camera could take photos in rapid succession, quickly catching a series of movements. Grandpa's pride and joy, my champion bull rider uncle, was built like a brick house with rigid muscle all the way from his fingers and fists, forearms, straight to his ears. Enormous cowboy wings extended down from his triceps to his lumbar and a rock-solid abdominal core. He looked like a superhero when he was travelling the rodeo circuit, always hungry for his next ride: enormous bulls and wild bucking horses for saddle bronc and bareback. After Grandpa bought that camera, he was constantly taking action shots of everything in sight. Everyone would gather around and look at Grandpa's newest shots; however, family favourites were always of Uncle.

"Hallo Sweetheart!" His voice, deep and cheery, calls from the kitchen. He honestly doesn't know it's me. He calls all of us girls "sweetheart." I walk into the kitchen and take a good, long look at him.

"Grandpa! Oh, there you are!" His eyes light up when he sees me. My eyes narrow when I see what is in front of him. He has his fork in hand and a big slice of apple pie. "Where'd you get the apple pie?" Grandpa is type 2 diabetic and takes insulin to balance his blood sugar levels.

"Granny's Kitchen." He loves his apple pie, although he's not supposed to eat things with too much sugar. There are pastry crumbs hanging off his whiskers.

"Ohh. Your favourite place, hey." His jaw clicks as he chews. I grab us each a glass of water and sit at the table with him. I am uncertain whether I should address his obvious transgression. Usually it is my aunties that talk to him about his sugar intake. "Hey Grandpa, listen to this!" He pauses for a moment and looks at me. I move my jaw, open and closed as though to chew: click, click, click. "Did you hear that? My jaw clicks too!"

"Mm-hmm." He pauses for a second and then has another bite. The crumbs are still dancing on the ends of his whiskers. I can't take my eyes off them. I sit for a minute watching and then start tidying his kitchen. Stack newspapers and old lottery ticket notations, wipe his old blue wooden table and stove, and then gather up dirty dishes. My young auntie walks in and she pauses to take a good, long look too. Grandpa continues to eat his pie.

"Dad, you're eating pie," she frowns at him. Grandpa ignores her and keeps chewing. Grandpa definitely knows he's eating apple pie, and he knows he's diabetic. He just really loves his pie, so he continues eating and the crumbs continue dancing on his whiskers. Auntie stares at me, and I raise my shoulders in confusion. I am the picture of innocence. My silent thoughts say, *I'm not his accomplice. Grandpa did this on his own.* She shakes her head and mutters her concern over his blood sugar levels. She joins me in gathering up his dishes, wiping down his counters.

"Mackie, come wash my windows." He gestures at me to come closer and hands me his eyeglasses.

"Okay, Grandpa." I lean forward so he can see my face. "I'm not my mom." Although I'm pretty sure he knows which granddaughter I am. Grandpa's middle name is Mack and he always calls my mom "Mackie."

"Oh…okay, Sweetheart." He squints at me and keeps eating.

Living with my sk̓ʷóz is good because now I visit Grandpa almost every day. I tell him stories of what I'm up to or who I've seen. He nods and his response is always, "Oh. That's good." If my sk̓ʷóz has been baking, I bring him a piece of her fresh-baked apple pie. One day I notice that his face is shifting from side to side as he talks. As he eats, it doesn't stop.

"Grandpa, why is your face shaky?" I ask, but he doesn't seem to understand what I'm talking about.

I don't know what to think about it, so I phone my young auntie because she lives right next door. When my young auntie walks in, she stands in the kitchen doorway and watches Grandpa. "Dad, what's going on? Why is your face shaking?" She immediately calls the community health nurse.

Grandpa was having a stroke and had to go to the hospital by ambulance. I felt bad that I didn't know the signs. I was sure glad my auntie arrived when she did. Though I observed the symptoms, I did not understand that they were the early signs of a stroke. After that, things changed. Due to his diabetes and his age, he couldn't live alone anymore. Grandpa, always so independent, moved into a bachelor suite in a building for seniors in town. He could still leave anytime he wanted but had to be back by nine o'clock in the evening. He bought a motorized scooter and every day he would cruise to his favourite spots: Quilchena Square and Granny's Kitchen.

I know I'm being a nuisance, but I keep dropping by to check on him almost every day. Sometimes I just want to look at him and make sure he's okay. If it's not me then it's one of my aunties. In the morning, I cook him mush; after school, I make him dinner. We all take turns washing his dishes and cleaning his bathroom. Sometimes I just respect his need for quiet, and I don't say anything at all. I clean, or I sit on the floor beside him when we watch television because he only has one chair. Sometimes, I sit and just listen to Grandpa breathe and watch him sleep.

People who remember her say my grandmother had a robust laugh. In pictures, she reminds me of my auntie. My grandmother was Syílx from Fish Lake. She had a brother and a sister living near Vernon, as well as several other siblings. Most of my grandmother's siblings are gone too. I didn't grow up knowing my grandmother's family although I met a few of them at family and community events. It was always wonderful when my mom and aunties and uncles got to visit her brother, Grand-Uncle Edward and her sister, Grand-Auntie Elizabeth. Old-school grit, lanky and tall, Grand-Uncle Edward remained a strikingly handsome Syílx cowboy. As a fluent Nsyílxcn speaker he orated great stories and always magically captured everyone's attention when he entered a room. My mom and all of her siblings must have been so sad when my grandma passed away.

My grandpa was proud to have fought on the front lines alongside his Canadian compatriots in World War II. Many Indigenous soldiers gave their lives fighting on the front lines for Canada. Like many others, he was treated as an equal overseas, but when he returned home, he faced racism. When Indigenous veterans returned, many were disenfranchised against their will, with no knowledge or understanding of the rights they had lost. That happened to my friend's grandpa. To be disenfranchised meant that the government removed their Indian status and all the associated rights according to the Indian Act. After they were disenfranchised, the person no longer had the right to live on reserve or own land on reserve even if that person was a status Indian according to the Indian Act. This happened to a lot of Indigenous men returning from the war. Indigenous women, and their children, were disenfranchised if they married a non-status man, even if he was

Indigenous. So, when my status mom married my Métis dad, she was disenfranchised.

The Canadian government's laws for Indigenous people are terribly confusing. The Indian Act, as implemented by the government for us "Indians" has so many multi-tiered laws and policies for colonizing and policing every element of our existence. There was a time when being disenfranchised meant Indigenous people were no longer allowed onto their home reserves, even to visit family. If the government disenfranchised the father, this impacted his whole family. If a non-Indigenous woman, white or other, married a status man, that woman and even her non-Indigenous children from previous relationships gained full Indian status. This law changed in 1985. At that time, my mom and I regained our status. The Royal Proclamation of 1763 is said to have established rules and protocols determining our "rights and freedoms" as Indigenous people. Ensuring that as "Indians" we should not be "molested or disturbed," and our rights to our land not abused. Yet across Canada, every inch of Indigenous land and waterways were stolen, molested, and disturbed as were Indigenous women and children, in conjunction with the decimation of our ancestors caused by colonial diseases. Indian reservations were created in locations that were deemed unworthy and uninhabitable by white euro-settlers. The Canadian government forcibly relocated many Indigenous communities across Canada to places with minimal to no accessible traditional resources that are critical to the abundant, healthy existence of the people, particularly clean drinking water, fishing, hunting, and the gathering of traditional foods and medicines.

I have heard stories about my grandpa when he came home from the war. At one point in his life, he was a violent man. Like my mom, both of my grandparents grew up in Indian Residential School. Grandpa was barely a young man when he went away and joined the Canadian Army. Then he came home and married my grandmother. Every single one of their nine children was taken away: the three oldest to St. George's Indian Residential School and the six youngest into the foster care system.

During the prohibition, the production of alcohol became a source of revenue. Alcoholism became an addiction. For my grandparents, Loved Ones, community members, alcoholism was how they coped with sorrow, hurt, rage, unresolved trauma, and the deep, overwhelming sense of powerlessness that began when they were children stolen from the safe, loving arms of their family. Many of our Loved Ones carry lifelong hurt and despair that is generations old. As Indigenous people we carry the burden of our ancestors, but we also carry their strength. Their courage. Their resilience.

I am not exactly certain how old I was when Grandpa decided to stop drinking. He was diagnosed with diabetes, and he was the first person in our family to stop. He never drank again, and I truly believe that was the best gift he could have given to all of my aunts and uncles and to his grandchildren. He was a hard-working, tireless man, and he loved all of his descendants. I loved my grandpa for the person that he was for all of us grandchildren.

Learning to Heal

My young mom scheduled an appointment at the Indian Friendship Centre in town. Eighteen years old, I've been looking for work and I'm willing to travel. I considered looking for work in Merritt, but aside from working as a chambermaid again, there aren't many options. I had a summer job at one hotel in Merritt when I was sixteen. The owner was gross and made passes at me when his wife wasn't there. I quit after that. When we drove through Jasper on our way to Edmonton to visit my dad's family, there were job postings stuck in store windows everywhere. Hotels, restaurants, cafés, ice cream stores, even the post office. I imagined that it would be an amazing adventure to move there for work. I had heard that the bigger hotels had staff houses for men and women. To wake up surrounded by the Rocky Mountains every morning, with herds of elk close by would be so cool. Change would be good. It's hard living in Merritt because everyone still remembers when I used to drink. I remember too. And I don't intend to drink ever again.

I walked past the Friendship Centre several times with only the yellow weeds paying witness to my stealth approach. First, eyeballing the office from the opposite side of the street, then being drawn closer by curiosity. I wanted to look in the windows. What solution would they have? Through the window I could see the receptionist sitting behind the desk. I felt nervous to enter through the glass doors.

"Hi, I have an appointment with a counsellor." The coolness of the room was a relief from the heat outside.

"Okay, I'll let her know you're here." The receptionist smiled. Seated on one of the brown, vinyl-upholstered seats, I read the posters on the walls. Images of Native youth and families all with Indigenous designs using red, yellow, black, and white, and pictures of animals: eagles, wolves, or whales. "Stop Smoking," posters of skeletons and rotten lungs for the national strategy to stop cigarette smoking. I saw these posters in the Kamloops Indian Friendship Centre too. Along with the same stack of newspapers in the corner: *Kahtou, Raven's Eye*, and *Windspeaker*, all Native newspapers.

"It takes a community to raise a child." Some of my best childhood memories are in the homes of my old mom, my aunties, Elders, and grand-aunties. Everything always tastes better when it's cooked with love: fresh baked bread, hamburger stew, fried bologna and rice, and of course, Red Rose tea with cream and lots of sugar.

I used to see a counsellor back at my high school in North Kamloops. I used to sit in his office. As much as I loved living with my grand-auntie, I had moved to Kamloops to finish grade eleven and twelve. Relocation was my solution for sobriety. My skʷóz made me want to become a better human being. I quit partying. I stopped drinking and moved away from old party friends and everyone who knew my favourite drinks. I wanted to change the direction of my life and graduate from high school.

There wasn't anything really special about the high school counsellor's office: plenty of stacks of papers and books on shelves. I have no idea what he looked like aside from the fact that he was non-Native. There was an awkward silence until I finally asked him, "So, um…I was wondering, about depression?" I had noticed a difference between my newest high school friend and me. How our minds work. She would blab on and on about what she was going through, but she never seemed to go to the dark places where I went.

"I wish I was dead. I wish I was dead. I wish I was dead. I wish I was dead." I wrote this on a piece of paper. I was angry. I was sad. I wanted to give up on life and I was just a kid. My mom had gone into the store. She was annoyed when she left and when she came back, she took the paper from me and read it. She was even more angry after that, or maybe it was hurt. Her solution was hollering and then silence. Silence driving from town to home; silence in the house; silence at the dinner table. I felt like a nothing, like a ghost. Just a big disappointment. In hindsight, I can't fathom why I would write something like that. Maybe it was the deep misunderstandings that silence brings? I felt unloved. Now that I am older, I imagine that she must have felt alone and unsupported as a mother. She was so young when she had me and my dad died only months later. My godmom would greet me with love and joy when she was hurting, when she was sick, even when she was suicidal. She said that losing her two kids in the house fire broke her heart. She said that I helped pick up those pieces and heal her broken heart. Both my birth mom and my godmom had broken hearts, but their hurt showed in different ways. And they expressed their love in different ways.

"Depression." He gave me an odd look, maybe curious but not judgmental. I've known plenty of cool teachers and plenty of judgmental teachers, including the principal. Ugh, her voice still repeats over and over in my mind.

"I'm part Native too, you know. Being Native is not an excuse for failure. Especially at your age." She was standing above me wearing her fancy suit. She wasn't like any Native person I ever knew. "Why did you move to Kamloops? You should've stayed in Merritt." I left her office feeling sick, like a loser and a failure. She reminded me of my mother on her bad days. I wanted to do well in school. I wanted to do "good" in life. The school principal was judgmental. The school counsellor was not.

"A lot of people think depression is a bad thing. To a certain extent, it is a normal reaction to certain events. The death of a loved one would be one example."

"Is it inherited? Like, if a person grew up around someone who was depressed and suicidal?"

"That's a good question. I would say as an unhealthy coping mechanism, it's learned. But learning new and healthy coping mechanisms is also possible."

"Learning new coping mechanisms? What's a 'coping mechanism'?"

"Well, a coping mechanism would be how you mentally and emotionally respond or cope with certain kinds of stress, hardships, or problems in your life."

"How can a person learn new coping mechanisms?"

"Well, first of all, it's important to understand that the brain is just like a muscle. It likes to recycle stuff, like old thoughts, old beliefs. For some reason the negative, self-deprecating thoughts are easiest to recycle. To be honest, it's not a good idea to believe everything your brain tells you, because the brain has a tendency to repeat negative thoughts." I sat back on the office chair, totally stumped.

Seriously, the brain is like a muscle? Oh my god. What is this guy talking about? I stared blankly at him as he continued.

"However, you can retrain your brain by constantly introducing positive affirmations and actively learning healthy coping skills."

"The brain is like a muscle? That's weird. Is depression normal for someone my age?"

"That's a tough question to answer. Depression is common for a lot of people, particularly those who have experienced childhood trauma. It is also important to remember there are different types of depression. Are you suicidal?" He paused and looked at me directly, waiting for my answer.

What should I tell him? I had thought about suicide, a lot. Suicide was my dark place, my alone place, a place where my mind went when I wanted to give up. When I felt truly unloved, unlovable, and worthless. It was the place where I went when my self-hate was unbearable. I felt unsure if I wanted to die or if I just wanted to stop feeling so worthless, so alone, and so unloved.

"I…uh…I don't know. I think I'm depressed though. I want to learn how to fix it. Should I see a doctor?"

"Seeing a doctor is definitely an option. Depending on the type of depression, a doctor might want to prescribe antidepressant medication. However, for some people, medication isn't the best answer. Changing your lifestyle and changing the way you think is another option. For example, learning new coping mechanisms. Also, seeing a therapist and committing to regular physical exercise are two more options. But let's talk some more about what's happening for you. You had mentioned that there have been a lot of changes in your life recently."

"Yes."

"Did you want to talk about some of those changes?" Apprehensive, I sat and pulled at loose threads on the old armchair.

"Well… I quit drinking, and I stopped hanging out with my old friends. That I, uh, used to party with. That's why I left home. I used to drink, a lot." Lately, Diane and I had been going dancing at Woods After Dark, a nightclub in Kamloops. It was fun. Grandpa helped me buy my first car, a Ford Escort. I was pretty certain it was because he didn't like me driving his old truck after it broke down on the old Kamloops Highway. My orphan benefit cheque was just enough to cover my whole car payment. And then I got a job waitressing at an italian restaurant on Tranquille Road. Diane doesn't really drink at all, so even though we go out on weekends, our fun times are always sober. Having fun sober is a lot more fun. I am never sick the next day, or worse, raped. There's no drama, no guys. No drunk crying. No more waking up hurt or ashamed. No one to give me booze or guilt me into drinking again. No one to drive me way up a mountain back road in the winter and tell me to have sex with him or get out.

Having a sober friend the same age as me changed everything. Drinking wasn't a problem for her. Alcohol wasn't a part of her conversation and neither was judgment. She had a wonderful grandma and her mom was always close by. If she did drink, it was maybe one then she would be sick. And she would go on and on about how sick she was. As a teenager, I drank beer the same way I ate popcorn—I could double-fist my Kokanee or Budweiser with a half sack hanging off of each wrist. Then drink every can and more.

"You indicated that you are room-and-boarding here in Kamloops. Where is your family?"

"My mom is…" My mom. "My mom and I don't really see eye to eye." My mom is a soldier, a warrioress surviving everything that life throws her way. When my aunties and uncles were all small and taken away to white foster homes, she used to walk all over the valley to visit them. She was just a kid. They were all kids. My mom's still on the front line, doing everything she can to survive, to change her life, our lives. That's what I think when I'm not mad at her anyway. "My mom, my baby brother, and my sister are living in Vancouver. She's going to UBC to finish her teaching degree." I must be a hard kid to love. I have too much attitude. I'm too emotional. It's too much work having me around. Thank goodness I have my godmom and my sk̓ʷóz. Truth is, I've learned to go house to house visiting aunties, Elders, and Loved Ones when I need love or a good lecturing. It's a lot easier to do that now I have a car.

"Why didn't you move to Vancouver with her?"

"Well I did when I was fourteen, but it didn't go well. I hated living in Vancouver. Then I started partying and arguing with my mom. I got kicked out a lot. I moved home. I tried living with my stepdad but that didn't work out and he kicked me out too. And then I was always drinking and partying in Merritt and…a lot of bad things happened."

"I see."

"Things are a lot better now that I've moved to Kamloops even though I'm on my own. My goal is to finish high school and graduate. To be honest, social studies and english just don't make sense. It's like, Native people aren't even part of the equation for British Columbia."

My First Nations counsellor at the Friendship Centre in Merritt was Nłeʔkepmx as well, but from Lytton, BC. She talked about healing from a First Nations perspective. She talked about cere-monies and the women's sweatlodge. All her yéyeʔs are Nłeʔkepmx. Like me, she grew up picking huckleberries and saskatoon berries. Sx̌ʷúsm, Indian ice cream, was one of her favourite things in the whole wide world, just like me. She understood me in a way the counsellor at Norkam Secondary didn't. And I liked how she explained the medicine wheel. Our youth group teacher for our creative writing group at the Kamloops Indian Friendship Centre taught us about writing poetry. He also explained how the four elements of the medicine wheel can help heal our lives. He made us create a circular diagram on a piece of paper and map out how our lives sit within the teachings of the medicine wheel.

The four quadrants of the medicine wheel are: mental, spiritual, emotional, and physical. I liked how the quadrants gave me a strategy for understanding my life. And, as my high school counsellor had explained, the medicine wheel helped me learn healthy coping mechanisms. I wrote lists in my journal under each heading. I wrote about the things in my life that were working and not working. Then I wrote a list of ways that I could change them.

Mental = mind
- School. I need to do better in school if I want to graduate.
- Math. I need a tutor.
- I hate english, but I enjoy reading fiction and fantasy fiction.
- I hate learning about people in europe. I hate learning about europe.
- I hate social studies too.
- To be honest, I want to learn about the true history of British Columbia.

Emotional = heart
- Emotional would be crying right? I definitely cry. A lot. I feel like a failure.
- The counsellor mentioned that seeing a counsellor helps work through emotional stuff.

- The counsellor also said that when one or two areas aren't as strong as other areas, then your medicine wheel goes off balance. That it affects your life, similar to how a flat tire affects a car. So a big part of the healing process is balancing all elements of the medicine wheel.
- This area is definitely a work in progress.

Physical = exercise
- What am I doing for exercise? Why is exercise important? Apparently, exercise causes a flow of natural happy vibes called endorphins, which is basically a natural antidepressant that exists inside your body (that's cool). The more you exercise the more energy you have and the stronger your body gets. And the more endorphins you naturally create. Through exercise, I can heal my heart. That's really cool. And I noticed if I go for a run, I sleep better. I feel happier.
- I hate baseball. I asked my phys. ed. teacher if I could run laps around the field instead of baseball. He said no. I even offered to run non-stop for the whole period, until PE was over. He still said no. I don't mind basketball and volleyball, but I hate standing in the middle of the field waiting for a stupid ball.
- I really like running. Maybe I should try going for more runs on my own time, after school. I run from one telephone pole to the next. Then when I'm tired, I walk to a telephone pole. Then I run to the next telephone pole. Every time I go for a run, I feel stronger, and my distance is increasing.
- Dancing is exercise too! Diane and I go dancing a lot so that's cool. I love dancing.

Spiritual = prayer or the sweatlodge or ceremony

- I am definitely not going to church. Ever. But I'll happily pray every day.
- What are some other spiritual things that I can do? I could go to the sweatlodge. One where I feel safe. One time, Auntie brought me to a women's lodge. I liked the women's sweatlodge. I felt safe there.
- Time spent with Elders, does that count as spiritual? I like spending time with Elders.
- Diane's grandma tells us to go to the water to brush ourselves off and pray. My godmom used to talk about doing that. Diane's grandma is wonderful. She's tiny and she has silver braids. Diane's mom and grandma also like travelling to winter ceremonies in the Okanagan. They said they will bring me with them the next time they go.

Happiness List:
1) Reading novels.
2) Running. Running in the rain.
3) Walking.
4) Biking.
5) Fishing is super fun!
6) Dinner with Grandpa and the whole family.
7) Hanging out with my cousins.
8) Time with Diane and her mom and grandma.
9) Time with my aunties.
10) Language classes and gathering traditional food with the Elders group.

i am sorry

i   betrayed   i   should have
    disrespected   listened
    hurt   respected
    you.   it was wrong.   believed
i   raped   protected
    assaulted   it was so   supported
    violated   terribly   accepted
    dishonoured   wrong.   loved
    you.   you.

                    i apologize
                  for my racism,
        for my discrimination. for my oppression.
        my behaviour was shameful. i am ashamed.

i didn't know   what to say.   i   ostracized
                what to do.   bullied
                how to help.   instead   belittled
                                    i lied.   hurt
                                                        hunted
you needed   love   i denied   lied
                compassion   what   betrayed.
                patience   happened
                                    to you.

i am   sorry.   you were   i was
i was   an enabler.   vulnerable
            cruel.   alone.
            afraid.   you broke me.
            confused.   i am broken.
            racist.

— 98 —

i carried　　　shame　　　inside me
　　　　　　　fear　　　　for my
　　　　　　　hurt　　　　whole life.
　　　　　　　rejection
　　　　　　　hatred
after all this time
　　　how do　i　move forward　　　after　　　trauma.
　　　　　　　we　move on　　　　　　　　　　betrayal.
　　　　　　　　　recover　　　　　　　　　　violence.
　　　　　　　　　start over　　　　　　　　　grief.
　　　　　　　　　let go
　　　　　　　　　　　　　　　how do i
the tears　　　i　　　　　　pick　　stop
won't stop　　am　　　　　　myself　the
falling.　　　hurting.　　　up.　　hurt.

　　　people say forget.　　　people say get over it.
　　　why can't i forget?　　　why can't i get over it?
　　　　i will never trust ever again.

enablers need to
　　　　　　STOP　　　　BULLYING　　　victims
　　　　　　　　　　　ENABLING　　　perpetrators

i will　　always remember　　the words & actions
　　　　never　　forget　　　　　　　of those
　　　　　　　forgive　　　　　　　　　　in denial.

IF YOUR ACTIONS　　　IF YOUR WORDS CAUSE
　　　deny truth　　　　　　more violence
　　　deny accountability　　more hurt
　　　deny justice　　　　　to the victim
　　　　　　　YOU ARE AN ENABLER. STOP!

— 99 —

Holding a perpetrator accountable does not indicate a
denial of love.

it's okay to   not forgive   please   ask for help
               forgive   practise self-care
               honour yourself
               honour your hurt
               honour your broken heart

when the burden becomes too much
                         a safe place
   find   a counsellor
                         healthy ways to overcome

please allow yourself to

cry cry cry cry   heal heal heal heal

                        go   for a run/hike/bike ride
                                      up the mountain
healing is possible   to the water
find ways to turn your suffering into strength   to the sweatlodge

                 sweat it out   learn to play again
       do   what it takes   reset
                your dunks   recharge
                the work   reactivate
                              resurgence

find   *a mentor*   *an Elder*   *a safe zone*   *a safe place to rest*   *body*
                                                        heart
                                                        mind
      be committed   to transformation   *spirit*

it is okay.

to never ever forgive.
it is okay to forgive.

it is okay to feel rage
for trusting the person
who caused so much pain

but

don't carry that burden for too long.

when you're ready.

let it go.

this does not mean denying justice. this does not mean denying accountability. this does not mean forgiveness. this means the burden of carrying hurt is too heavy. the burden of carrying betrayal is too much. the definition is yours to make. the burden is not yours to carry.

write it. wrap it up. burn it. run it over 1000x. put it inside a punching bag. punch the ever-living crap out of it. tie it to an eagle feather. wrap it inside a bundle of broadcloth. put it inside a cedar box. bury it. wrap it in cedar boughs. wrap it in fir boughs. weave sweetgrass around it. place the bundle in the heart centre of the tree. place it in a ceremonial fire. paddle it across the water. carry it to the top of a distant mountain. put it away.

the tree. the flames. will carry your pain, your prayers to the creator. don't look back. don't turn and pick it up again.

put the shame away. don't carry it anymore. put it within a circle of stones. give it prayers. it is safe to speak the words when your witnesses are stone. name the stones. sadness. sickness. sorrow. betrayal. ask the good Grandfathers, good Grandmothers for help. return the stones to the water. this is your putting away ceremony.

we love you. we always loved you. we always will love you. no matter what. we honour you. we will walk with you. we are here for you. we will guide you as you heal. we will walk with you as you transform. we will always love you. you are worthy. of love. of kindness. of dreams. of language. of culture. of spirit. of setting goals. of achieving goals. of true joy. of protection. of self-protection. of nourishment. of silence. of solitude. of peace. of courage. of success. of self-care. of beauty. of passion. of health. of pleasure. of laughter. of strength. of respect. of compassion. of self-love. no matter what. no matter what. you are worthy.

there is a sacred place within you. that is where the spirit lives. that is where your child inside lives. deep within your being. wrap your arms around it. rock it. feed it love.

your spirit is power.
you are radiant.
you are love.

the same as trees

i remember the Elders
    talking to us as youth:
    at youth conferences, youth groups,
    at the sweatlodge.

they said:
    remember
    we human beings
    are the same as trees.

        cedar, douglas fir, pine, cottonwood:
        tree medicine. tree spirits.
        if you listen carefully in the high mountains
        you can hear the ancients sing.

today, our youth live in two worlds:
our traditional way and that of white society.
at times this will be confusing.
at times you may experience despair.
you will have to learn a new kind of strength.

        when i finally found my way there. to the sweatlodge.
        i was confused. i did not understand.

        two worlds: yes.

        i didn't understand this, "new kind of strength."
        how would i find it? from whom?

they said:
  if you choose to go away to learn, then do that
  but always return.
  if you are scared to take risks, then be scared
  and do it anyway. be stubborn. be persistent.
  have faith, have reverence, have compassion.

  i went away to learn. and i was afraid
  to fail. and i did fail: math. history. english.
  their history. their language.
  i wanted to quit.

remember:
  the blood flowing through you is the blood of our ancestors.
  sacred Grandmothers and Grandfathers who never gave up—
  even when our Loved Ones were buried in mass graves,
  even when the children were stolen. they persevered.
  this resilience exists within you.

  i didn't know our ancestors were buried in mass graves.
  our beautiful pit houses collapsed with entire families buried within.
  i often wondered how the blanket of despair came to us.
  i only knew the blanket was old,
  older than me. older than our family.
  i didn't know until I read the stories in books.

they said:
  as you go forward be that tree
  rooted deeply within our traditional homelands,
  grounded within our culture, nurtured by our Elders'
  teachings, ceremonies, and languages,
  woven within the skills and education of today's society.

raise your arms like branches, in strength and humility,
season to season weathering storms and heavy winds:
praying, cultivating knowledge,
ever growing, ever producing,
ever healing, ever dropping seeds and fertilizing.
in honour of our Elders, our culture,
our past and future generations.

for all things, there is a life cycle.
death in autumn and winter,
rebirth in spring, growth through summer.

> *standing among trees on a mountain trail*
> *searching for the string that tied my spirit to an earth*
> *i no longer wanted to walk.*
> *the year following my younger brother's death*
> *i remembered the words of my Elders.*

> *shoes off, toes immersed in creek, soil, sand & stones*
> *hands uplifted to the sky i emulated*
> *the patience of a tree, an ancient one rooted,*
> *needle tips or leaves, branches dancing with the breeze.*
> *perhaps their greatest pleasure is savouring raindrops,*
> *their greatest joy lifting sorrow, sickness.*

what generation are we?
  we are the transforming generation.
  we watched our parents and grandparents
  at war with themselves.
  empty bottles broken on the floor, scars
  too often on bloodied faces:
  our mothers and our grandmothers,
  our fathers and our grandfathers.
  as children, we learned church prayers.
  late at night when our parents didn't know
  we could hear our mothers weeping
  we prayed for their safety.
  we prayed to fix their broken hearts.

    i never understood her silence, followed her room to room.
    i felt unloved. unwanted.
    invisible.

    later i realized, as a survivor, the hurt she carried
    was so much deeper than i could understand.
    my elders and my godmother:
    always lit up, took care of me when she was broken.

    i remember her courage when she changed her life.
    as her oldest child, every day i prayed
    that we could be friends,
    learn how to be a mother and daughter.

as child witnesses, we watched a return to the old ways.
we watched as they put shame aside, remembering, relearning,
reawakening ancient traditional practices. we listened
as they taught us to talk to the spirit of our ancestors.

as they, now we, gain contemporary education, training.
we master ourselves. we gain control of our future.

> *it is time to lift those blankets of despair,*
> *put it all away. generations of*
> *suffering. grief. rage. suicide. violence.*
> *stop recreating and reliving genocide.*
> *it is time to put their shame away.*

what generation are we?
  we are the transforming generation.
  hands joined with our elders we help them heal and
  transform their sorrow into strength,
  in so doing, we heal and transform ourselves.

  hands joined we gift weavings of sacred memories,
  traditional practices, knowledge, and education,
  forward to future generations:
  our children and our children's children.

> *pray, sing, dance*
> *in ceremony, in celebration*
> *resurgence is our right.*
> *resurgence is our destiny.*

Land
Teachings

Métis

hardwood floors,
walls lined with books,
staircase: narrow and steep.

in matching red plaid pajamas,
we are twenty toes up, bellies warm
with ginger and lemon tea,
sweet with honey.

i want to be strong like her,
graceful like her.
i lay in her tiny house in Saskatoon,
memorizing:

her voice rich with Michif and Cree,   Indigenous languages
road allowance memories
the bent wisps of her hair.

read memories: a moose in her window,
a house without running water.

lived memories: a perfect black and white wood cookstove
within a valley of grass and poplar trees.

the river that took my father flows fast nearby

Beginnings
With Maria Campbell

Auntie says:
you are a fourth generation Red River Métis.
your dad's grandfather's mother was Mariah Vandal.
she was a great-niece to Gabriel Dumont.
Isadore Dumont was Gabriel Dumont's father and
he was the first casualty of the Riel resistance in 1885.

Colin Campbell was a Hudson's Bay Factor.
a fourth-generation halfbreed.
he was your dad's grandfather's father,
of Cree and Scottish descent.

and Chief Mistawasis of treaty 6
had a granddaughter, her english name was Irene.
her French halfbreed husband was a Dubuque.   family name
she was your paternal grandmother's mother.

listening,
i sit in silence and contemplate
beginnings and ancestral memory

a rainbow of thread,
weaving cultures,
weaving nations,
weaving blood,
weaving origins
makes the sash a story

of blood, of battles along
the south Saskatchewan shore

before Canada was Canada.

Prayer Warriors

"Nickle is coming home!"
her Secwepmx voice on the telephone
echoes his thoughtful questions:
"which day will she get here?"
"what are the ingredients?"

they are: Elders, storytellers, prayer warriors.
she is Secwepmx. he is Syílx.
at her table tea leaves flow.

"Saskatoon to Edmonton = one day.

Edmonton to Kamloops = one day.
two days, probably late afternoon."

"Crisco, flour, baking powder, one egg,
brown sugar and a tablespoon of vinegar.
apples and cinnamon.
my auntie's recipe," i explain.

the highway is blue over a long grass prairie.
in my rear-view a funnel cloud dances
a twirling doorway from sky to tmíxʷ.
my car achieves lightspeed travelling west,
a lone silver bullet across the prairie.

sister rivers sing me home
where pine trees and fragrant sage hills unfold.

in the doorway, my dear Elders stand side by side.
"Nickle! he wants you to bake apple pie.
all the ingredients are inside."

pleased, he leans on his cane,
a ray of light across his face,
ripe, red Okanagan apples sit close by.

gathering

we

ride the

school bus

like children,

kżéʔ, spápzeʔ, ʔímc.

Elders among descendants.

nɬeʔkepmxcín and nsyílxcn

is all that we hear. our languages,

yet younger generations do not understand.

air springtime crisp summer warmth gathering

we exit the school bus onto pine-cushioned ground

spápzeʔ breaks the tip of the jack pine, brilliant green

sweet with the nectar of spring. sunlit shadows dance among

pine and cottonwood trees, our ancestors join us on this day:

ancient like ɬəʔpnteʔ and sxéxeṅx, sacred like kʷátɬp and sḱepẏéɬp

ancient like mushrooms and stones, sacred like cedar and sḱepẏéɬp.

qálex̣ in hand we dig for the ɬkʷəpn whose roots wake and grow within this earth.

the texture and scent of soil and dust
sifted between fingers imprints upon our palms.
i am fool
to think
the blood
flowing
in my veins
is mine.

gathering songs

windows open wide
cruising mountain roads across our Scw̓éxmxuym̓x^w   territory of the
this little Ford rides low   People of the Creeks
full with yéyeʔs.

spíləx̣m echoes   remembered stories
of spring harvest and new shoots.
every springtime the land sings
beckoning our grandmothers to visit

scáq^wm blossoms unfold blessings   saskatoon berries
on the awakening land
springtime hungry,
on tiptoes we step across

minuscule tətúwṅ blossoms   wild potatoes
blooming on a bed of soil and pine,
blades of greenery: grass, c̓ewéteʔ, nodding onions.   wild celery
side by side like sisters: arrowleaf balsamroot and arnica.

blackened fingers sift and till grains of tmíx^w
pluck sweet tətúwṅ
potato berries from the dust and
return long, pink worms to their cultivation.

we seek you our ancestor, k̓ʷməm'i?me? sqáyxʷ   little man
you are łk̓ʷəpn, you are spíƛ̓m: bitterroot
bitter red heart roots weaving gossamer threads.
tenderly we tug your arms and legs from the land
while your pink blossom face sleeps, tightly folded.

we sing to you our stories,
sing to you our gathering songs.
we sing you into our deer stew and nkéxʷ   bitter pudding—
then sit patiently as you cook.   traditional dessert

this is our spring devotion ceremony
honouring our ancestors
feeding our children
the riches of our land,

tmíxʷ

sn'ix'wam

Creator, sacred pole,
four sacred directions,
Grandmothers, Grandfathers,
with you we eat, with you we pray,
give thanks, have giveaway.

little girls in wing dresses,
scarves, moccasins, and wispy braids.
little boys in ribbon shirts,
moccasins, Wrangler jeans.

soft hands, small feet on tiptoe
hands raised, singing,
around the sacred floor we go

in honour of all living things:
the swimmers, the four-legged,
the ones that crawl, the ones that fly,
the plants, the trees, the bushes.

roots, berries, trees, wildflowers,
sweet spring water
salmon, kokanee, ling cod,
deer, moose, bumblebees, rattlesnakes,
eagles, bluebirds, frogs.

medicine for body.
medicine for mind.
medicine for spirit.

this is who we are.
this is how we live.
this is how we pray.

pain hurt rejection left behind
nurturing acceptance love joy ceremony
among Loved Ones and ancestors.

Coming to My Senses

The land, we are woven together like strands of light

Every day I sit wearing headphones connected to a transcription machine while unseen voices narrate stories about the land. My fingers rat-a-tat-tat across my keyboard, transforming traditional oratures to written words on my computer screen. The recorded interviews are often at a Chipmunks pitch as I play, rewind, fast-forward, and replay tape after tape.

My previous employment as Language and Culture Assistant at Nicola Tribal Association provided me with experience in transcription using the International Phonetic Alphabet. Knowledge of the Nɬeʔkepmxcín language and courses undertaken at the Nicola Valley Institute of Technology got my foot in the door for a job with the Aboriginal Rights and Title Department at Stó:lō Nation. My new job as transcriber for the Traditional Use Study (TUS) requires the verbatim transcription of interviews with Stó:lō Elders, Knowledge Carriers, and language speakers. Stories that document the traditional and contemporary use of the land and the way the Stó:lō, the "People of the River," live. The language spoken by the Stó:lō is Halq'eméylem. There are three main dialects: Halq'eméylem is what is spoken in the Fraser Valley and. Hənq'əmińəm' is spoken on the coastal mainland along the Fraser River including Musqueam. Hul'q'umi'num is spoken by Coast Salish people on Vancouver Island. I have learned that there are many, many different languages in BC and basically every village has its own subdialect within the dialect.

I find a friend on the first day at my new job. Her office is across the hall from mine in what at one time was the nurses' residence for the Coqualeetza Hospital. I knew she was wondering who the strange Native was because every time she walked by, she would peek in my door until I finally introduced myself. I jokingly told her my office sink was available for her use anytime she wanted and if she ever needed to find me, I would be in the closet. Apparently, my office was originally a janitor closet. Ever look into another person's eyes and instantly see kindness there? Her eyes are like that. She has an amazing laugh. She shares an office with her boss—they are working on employment and training projects. Their service delivery area extends all the way from Yale to Coquitlam and Surrey. They also work with Indigenous communities along BC's Northwest Coast.

The offices are located on the grounds of what was once the Coqualeetza Indian Institute, also referred to as the Coqualeetza Indian Residential School. Many of the buildings on the original site have been demolished due to deterioration and aging construction; others have been renovated and new buildings have been added to suit the evolving needs of the surrounding Stó:lō community. The Coqualeetza Indian Residential School opened in 1894 in Sardis, British Columbia. Sardis is directly across Highway 1 from Chilliwack, although Sardis is now referred to as Chilliwack. In 1940, the residential school was converted to the Coqualeetza Indian Hospital and reopened in 1941. Indigenous people from throughout British Columbia with tuberculosis and other infectious diseases were cared for at the Coqualeetza hospital. Although it became known as one of the only fully accredited hospitals in the Fraser Valley, the care it provided Indigenous people was still segregated and inadequate. The Canadian government maintained "ownership" of the grounds and all the buildings until the hospital closed in 1969. At that time, they intended to transfer ownership of the Coqualeetza site to the Canadian Military. However, when the Stó:lō chiefs found out, they refused to allow that transfer to happen. They occupied the entire site and demanded ownership. The Stó:lō reclaimed the entire Coqualeetza grounds, and the government and army eventually conceded. Ownership of the entire Coqualeetza site, including all the buildings, was signed over to the Stó:lō.

I'd heard my Elders from home talk about Coqualeetza and Sardis many times, but I never understood the significance. Sometimes they spoke of the Coqualeetza Indian Residential School and when the school became a hospital. They often told stories of those Loved Ones who had extensive stays in the hospital due to tuberculosis and other illnesses. Too often, they had unanswered questions about the many children that never returned.

In 1973, under the mandate of twenty-four Stó:lō chiefs, Coqualeetza became incorporated as a non-profit charitable organization. The Elders from my home territory spoke highly about the Coqualeetza Cultural Education Centre because of how inspiring and progressive their language and cultural programs were in the 1970s and 1980s. This included the Halq'eméylem language classes, the development of the Halq'eméylem writing system, and the archival and curriculum development work they were doing. At that time, the work they were doing was considered super transformational all across Indian Country and inspired the development of language and cultural programs within Indigenous communities throughout British Columbia.

As a youth, I often listened to my Elders' conversations as they reminisced. I didn't understand why Indian Residential School had such a huge impact on our lives. I thought it was just a school, like the one I attended. The difference was that everyone, including my mom and Grandpa, had to live there. I didn't realize that every single baby and child in our whole family and community was taken. I didn't understand that the Canadian government and churches forcefully ripped apart every single Indigenous family and community across Canada for the purpose of "severing all ties" the children had to their parents, making them forget their traditional territories and culture in order to, "kill the Indian in the child." As a child, I didn't understand that thousands of Native children died in those schools. I didn't know that every single Indian Residential School in Canada had a graveyard. Nor did I know about the horrific abuse and violence, not to mention neglect and starvation that Indigenous children endured while they stayed there. My Elders said they didn't grow during the months of school. When the children returned home for the summer and resumed their nutritious traditional diet, that was when they went through tremendous growth spurts. It is hard to imagine the devastation felt by the children that were forced to stay in those schools year-round.

I had questions: Why did Indian Residential School continue to have such a grip on how our people lived and functioned? Why didn't we learn about the true history of Indian Residential Schools and the Canadian government policies surrounding them in elementary and especially high school? Following graduation, I took post-secondary courses at the Nicola Valley Institute of

Technology in Merritt, courses that explained the discriminatory nature of Canadian government policies and how they impacted Indigenous people. I remembered my Elders sharing experiences of having every single tooth pulled from their mouths by dentists. Even perfectly healthy teeth were replaced with a full set of dentures. When instructors became courageous enough to teach beyond the discriminatory, oppressive, and racial bias of the status quo, that was when we began to learn the true history of Canada. When schools actually became schools and not oppressive institutions, that is when they began to teach the minds and hearts of the children and people.

Another new friend is Amy. Amy shares stories about her experiences as a university student. She works closely with my two supervisors. All three of them are non-Native and straight out of university. Amy has a bachelor's degree in forestry from the University of Victoria and a master's degree in environmental resource management from the University of Manitoba. The other two have their archaeology degrees from McGill University and the University of British Columbia. There's also a genealogist, an archivist, and several other non-Native staff with degrees. There are several Indigenous TUS team members: the interviewers and the transcribers. As far as I know, none of the Indigenous employees have thus far completed a post-secondary degree.

I like it here. I like learning about Stó:lō culture. I like this feeling of starting over because everything in my life is brand new. I had a long-term relationship, but I wasn't ready to be a wife. There were days when it was fun, but I came to a point where I felt trapped and I stopped growing. Now that I am seeing what everyone else in the world is doing, I feel as though I have a chance at achieving something in life. It makes me want to dream for something more, but not just dream; it makes me want to work towards achieving my dreams. Laughter is echoing down the long hallway. One thing about these Stó:lō women is they sure can laugh. They laugh loud and long just like my mom and aunties when they get together and they are happy.

Tina is my newest co-worker and newest friend. Tina is small, and her shoulders are broad and strong. Every day after work she goes to canoe practice, even when it's pouring rain. She's invited me to try out. I have refused every offer. "I'll get you on the canoe, just wait and see. Then you'll never want to get off!" We've had this same discussion every day. Canoe racing is most definitely a Stó:lō sport. Back home you'd be considered insane for going to the water in March unless it was between rounds at the sweatlodge or for ice fishing. Most people no longer go to the water in the winter.

My godmom said our people used to bathe in the creek or river right through the winter. They would just have to break through the ice. When she was young, her grandpa would wake her up before the sun rose and she would have to run to the creek. She said she would have to face the sunrise and brush herself off with fir boughs. The small river by her old house is sluggish and dirty. The lake and its tributary are now thick and green with milfoil. The result of being beside one of the biggest cattle ranches in Canada. In Stó:lō territory, the water is crystal clear and glacial blue. I've gone for winter baths at the women's sweatlodge with my Elder. Her crystal-clear creek is glacier-fed from the Similkameen Mountains. My godmom said the water has to be clear and fast-moving, not still or sluggish and dirty. If the water is still, it doesn't wash the negative energy away.

We both have our headphones on, but Tina and I continue bantering between tapes. Foot off the transcription machine pedal then a light tap to rewind. "Are you kidding? Me on a canoe? You've gone mad." I shake my head, thinking, goodness sakes, this woman really doesn't know me the way I know me.

Her hands and feet are busy, like mine. "That's what you say right now but come on, just try it once, okay?"

"HA! What a laugh that would be! I'm like a cat when it comes to water!"

"Technically, you aren't in the water, you're on a canoe. You're above the water. The only time we're actually in the water is when we carry the canoe from the beach to the water and then get in."

"Aside from the 99% of the time when it's raining. I'll watch but I'm not paddling. Not ever. Never, ever. Have you looked outside? It's not even spring yet! It's cold outside and there's still snow in the mountains!" Grey sky. The rain is relentless. Rain all day, rain all week; it has literally been raining for months. The darkness and low clouds never leave. I started taking vitamin D to help offset the depression ever-looming along my periphery. She stares at me and then rolls her eyes.

"You're stronger than you think you are. You'll be fine."

"Okay, okay, I'll go check it out. But don't think that I'm going to get on." Tina laughs. Foot on the pedal, I give her the sideways furry eyeball.

"Ha! You don't scare me!" She laughs again.

I used to swim and play in the lake all day when I was a kid. But now like a cat I stand along the shore, pacing. My Elders said it is important to pray at the water. I do my four dunks, but I don't play in the water anymore. I am constantly aware of the water's ability to take lives. Whenever anyone talks about the loss of a parent, I understand the emptiness. It didn't bother me as much when I was a kid, but something changed inside me. If I could describe it in words, I would say growing up without a dad is like a constant state of wandering. It is a deep feeling of disconnectedness with a constant yearning to be rooted as a daughter. A constant yearning for the everlasting safety and security of unconditional love, yet never finding it. I am an intergenerational survivor of residential school. Is it possible that all survivors of trauma feel this sense of disconnectedness? Maybe it is because I imagined a perfect ideal, that a biological dad would bring connectedness, a playful sense of humour and warm, loving arms. A place where I would always feel truly loved, safe, and protected. I am learning truths though, that as a result of residential school, the Sixties Scoop, and colonization—dads everywhere are struggling to recover from their own hurt, too. Like bundles, dads carry the memories of their childhood, deep inside. And like the rest of us, it emerges when they least expect it. Even so, I want to belong to a dad.

tmíxʷ. temexw. temxulaxʷ.

when the colonizers arrived
they stole everything beautiful
our children. our languages.
our land. our water.
songs, stories, ancestral memories.
desecrated sacred ceremonies.

presented gifts of disease, addiction, shame
destroyed and prohibited all things
woven of the land:
harvests of medicinal and berry plants, roots, tea
blankets, regalia, baskets, carvings.
stole our food—replaced it with
flour, sugar, alcohol, contaminated traders, blankets
carrying smallpox, influenza, tuberculosis.

now we put the blankets of hurt away.
rip apart rotten diseased strands
tattered, torn from years of decay
strip away strands of embodied trauma
decrepit racist colonial hate.

put it in the fire
bury it in a box
bring it to the water
return to sacred ancestral memories.

grandmother sister daughter
grandfather brother son
resurgence awakens
the healing energy within.

the weavers return
when the trees awaken
from a deep winter sleep
activated by the flow
of sap in spring.

when the weavers arrive
the trees are singing: roots, trunk, branches
sway all the way to the sky,
remembered gentle spirits—reverent touch
of those harvesting reciprocating love.

gathering washing spinning
twining warping vital strands
wool cedar spruce bark roots
pine needles Indian hemp sweetgrass

temxulaxʷ tmíxʷ temexw
weave ourselves back together
all that is sacred
hearts spirits minds bodies
earth wind sky water
life force spirit languages.

we are the land
where our languages emerge
we are here. we have always been here.

Nłeʔkepmxcín. Nsyílxcn.
Secwepemctsín.
Sťáťimcets.
Hul'q'umi'num. Halq'eméylem. Hənq'əminəm'.
Tsleil-Waututh. Skwxwú7mesh sníchim.
Xʷməθkʷəy'əm. Quw'utsun.
Tla'amin. Éy7á7juuthem.
SenćoŦen. She shashishalhem.
Tsilhqot'in. Tse'khene. Tutchone.
Wetalh. Dakelh. Gitxsanimx.
Wit'suwit'en. Nedu'ten. Nisga'a.
Sgüüxs. Smalgyax.
Xaaydaa Kil. Xa"islakala.
Kwakwaka'wakw.
Ktunaxa.
Diiʔdiitidq. Nuxalkmc. Wuikinuxv.
Nuučaańuł. Haíłzaqv.
Tāłtān. Łingít.
Dene-Zaa. Danezāgé'.

weave ourselves back together
sacred strands of light and dark
woven fibres filaments of
motherhood fatherhood
birthing raising empowered children.

compassion, forgiveness, safety.
fundamentals of culture, family, truth
peace, joyful play, laughter,
self-discipline and love.

sacred rememberers. orators.
educators. ancestral narratives.
pedagogies for traditional education.
cultural and spiritual practices.
matriarchs and warriors.
communities, families, children
the soil of British Columbia.

Pit house people.
River people.
Village people.
Longhouse people.
Ocean people.
Big house people.
The original humans
of this land.

temxulax^w. temexw. tmíx^w.
embedded intertwined

the land, we are
woven together
like strands of light.

the land remembers.

Porcupine Song

Witnessing the Stó:lō chiefs' meetings and learning about the Treaty process and the research undertaken by the Aboriginal Rights and Title Department gave me a lot of appreciation for the magnitude of work necessary to transform our communities and our Nations across British Columbia and Canada. Healing and transformation needs to occur from within ourselves, within our families, and within our communities. At the meetings, chiefs and hereditary leadership, young and old, male and female, sit together; each takes their turn listening and speaking. The meeting rooms are always full to capacity even when the room is half empty. If I had 3D glasses that detected ancestor spirits, I am certain I would see the ancestors of these leaders standing among them.

Our Elders, matriarchs, and visionaries gave everything they had, strategizing to create positive change all across Canada and British Columbia, regardless of laws preventing organized gatherings. In Stó:lō territory, the people stood together against the government and reclaimed Coqualeetza. I'm not saying they didn't have negative internal dynamics; just like every other community, they did; however, they persevered with tremendous love in their hearts for the land and the people. They set goals. They developed working groups and worked from the ground up. They struggled but they found ways to continue moving forward. Community wellness and self-determination, governance of health, wellness, land and water stewardship, economic development ventures, and child and family services are just a few areas in which Indigenous leaders and communities are systematically and tenaciously making progress. They do so while preserving a deep reverence for their children, Elders, families, culture, spirituality, and traditional governance practices. The structure and organization of how they do business in accordance with Stó:lō protocol makes the work they do even more beautiful. It is reciprocal and interconnected, and everything is intrinsically embedded with cultural and spiritual values and practices. It keeps the work focused on love for their future generations, family, community, and traditional territory. Stó:lō protocol: the calling of witnesses, the blanketed orator, the hundreds of hand drums on the floor; this process is unlike anything that I've ever witnessed in my home territory.

It is a strange feeling to realize how vastly different yet similar each of our Nations is in British Columbia. There are almost forty Indigenous languages spoken in British Columbia and many of those languages have significant dialectal variations depending on the region and village. In elementary and high school, I didn't learn about Interior Salish or Coast Salish people, our languages, or all of the Indigenous Nations of British Columbia. We learned minimal details about the people from Haida Gwaii and Eastern Canada. For example, how "Canada" was supposedly adapted from the Iroquois word, kanata.

Pit house people. River people. Longhouse people. Ocean people. Big house people. Our ancestors designed, built, and lived in traditional homes while providing for their families and communities. Carriers of sacred ancestral knowledge, carriers of cultural and spiritual practices. Powerful, beautiful songs, images, and artistic designs. Thousands of villages. Generations of people: communities, families, children. Indigenous DNA as ancient as the soil we walk upon is embedded within every corner of this tmíxʷ now called British Columbia.

Salish, Interior Salish, and Coast Salish are colonial terms used to refer to the Indigenous people that reside in what is now known as the Southern Interior and West Coast British Columbia all the way down into Washington State. Sometimes subtle, most often dynamic, linguistic variations differentiate one group from the next. Languages, communities, cultures, and spiritual practices are not a reflection of pop culture and what is currently "cool"; they reflect the landscape and waterscape, and they are directly linked to the spirits that exist within each of our traditional territories.

As the people of the Nicola Valley, we are considered to be Interior Salish, of the Nłeʔkepmx linguistic group, which includes the Southern Interior Plateau Region and Northern Cascades. The people of the Nicola Valley are often referred to as Scwéxmx, "People of the Creeks." My Elders have jokingly stated that we are referred to as "People of the Creeks" because our Nicola and Coldwater rivers are so much smaller than the Thompson and Fraser rivers that unite in Lytton, BC. There are stories of an Athapaskan people who came to the Nicola Valley and resided among the Nłeʔkepmx and Syílx people of this valley. But not much is known about them and why they came or how long they stayed. It has been said many times by our Elders that those who didn't die during the epidemics were absorbed into our community.

According to the Indian Act, there are five "Indian Bands" in the Nicola Valley, and each of these Indian Bands is made up of many Indian Reserves, which are numbered (e.g., "IR #"). Four of the Indian Bands are Nłeʔkepmx. The Coldwater Indian Band has their main reserve below the Coquihalla Highway. It is cooler in the mountains than the valley bottom. The Coldwater River, ćałetkʷu, flows through the Coquihalla Mountains from the west into the town of Merritt and joins the Nicola River; together they travel to the Thompson River. By the Mamette Lake turnoff, just north of the town of Merritt, is Sptétxw, or Springs Reserve. This is where my great-grandparents, grandpa, and numerous grand-aunts and grand-uncles worked the land and built their homes with their families. My grandpa also owned land on Joeyaska Reserve. The Coquihalla Highway travels through my grandfather's land. Ownership of this land was passed to Grandpa's descendants when he passed away. Joeyaska, Springs, and Shulus are part of the Lower Nicola Indian Band. Further downriver is Nwéyc, which is the traditional place name for the "Nooaitch" Indian Reserve and the Nooaitch Indian Band. Sxéxenx, a place name meaning "little rocks falling," is the traditional name for the Shackan Indian Band. The place where the Nicola River joins the much larger Thompson River is Cook's Ferry Indian Band.

Quilchena and Spaxomin, or also known as the Upper Nicola Indian Band, is made up of Syílx people. It starts along the eastern shores of the Nicola Lake and goes up to Douglas Lake, through to what is referred to as Fish Lake or Salmon Lake. The weather is usually colder up Spaxomin because it is at a higher elevation. My maternal grandmother and maternal great-grandparents are Syílx from up Spaxomin. Our Syílx family extends all the way through Armstrong, BC to the Head of the Lake and Vernon, BC.

The majority of the Nicola Valley is inhabited by speakers of Nłeʔkepmxcín and then Nsyílxcn. At one time it was common to have orators who spoke five or more languages. Some of these included Nłeʔkepmxcín, Nsyílxcn, Secwepemctsín, Státimcets, and other Salish languages as well as english. As our Elders who are fluent speakers leave us, there are fewer and fewer people who speak even one Indigenous language. Many families are interconnected through marriage. For instance, within my families' ancestral lineage, one of our great-great-grandfathers was Chief Nk'wala. He had five wives. Each of those wives had many children and those families and descendants are extensive. Another example would be my great-grandparents who together had twelve children. My grandpa was the father of nine children and his siblings each had as many as fifteen children. Our blood lineage has direct linkages to many of the Nłeʔkepmx and Syílx families in the Nicola Valley, the Fraser Canyon through the Similkameen, the Okanagan Valley, and beyond.

From what I understand, my family name, Shuter, was adapted from the Nłeʔkepmx name Séwtaʔ, which is pronounced like "Shuta." Many of our traditional names were lost through Indian Residential Schools and their name registries. Many Indigenous names are gone forever due to generations of files that were lost or destroyed by Indian Agents, Indian Residential School staff, and by fires. Names that connected us to our ancestors were changed to names from the bible and even the names of employers. The very first great-grandfather to receive an english name, such as Joseph, well that first name became the last name of all his descendants. Loss of names, loss of language, stolen identities; how can we ever know who we truly are if we do not know the true names of our ancestors? Many of our Elders say that our true state is the state of the spirit and that during ceremony and prayer, the Creator answers to our ancestral names. If our ancestral names are wiped away or forgotten, how will our ancestors recognize us once we cross over to the spirit world? How can I recognize myself?

Almost twenty years ago now, the Douglas Lake Cattle Company stopped allowing members of the Spaxomin community, or

"Upper Nicola Indian Band," to access sections of the ranch where, since the Douglas Lake Cattle Company came into existence, access had always been given. In response, the Upper Nicola Band held a huge roadblock, denying the Douglas Lake Cattle Company vehicles access to travel on the main road that passed through Upper Nicola Reserve land. In order to travel into the town of Merritt, or access any major highway, travel through the reserve is required. The only other option is a dirt road that leads to Armstrong, located between Kamloops and Vernon, BC. This route, depending upon destination, can add as much as four to five hours of travel time.

This event occurred in response to the actions of the Douglas Lake Cattle Company when they tried to deny the inherent rights of the original inhabitants. These actions are not just about the annual harvest of food sources; they are about the sacred responsibility to nurture, monitor, protect, honour, have ceremonies, and respect our Indigenous food sources, so that the land remains healthy for future generations. Indigenous rights to traditional resources such as fish, wildlife, and plants for food and medicine are non-negotiable, regardless of non-Indigenous ideologies on rights and access. Eventually, through respectful negotiation, consultation, and a court order, the Douglas Lake Cattle Company recognized and chose to honour the inherent rights of the Spaxomin people.

People don't say a lot about it, but the rivers and creeks downstream from the Douglas Lake Ranch have become stinky, brown, and polluted as a result of cattle runoff. This has affected the spawning grounds of the kokanee (a landlocked species of sockeye salmon), the rainbow trout, and the ling cod (also called burbot). Our ancestors nurtured and protected the land and waterways and then harvested strategically to allow for continual abundance, generation after generation. Fish, such as the kokanee, remain a main source of sustenance and continue to be harvested and preserved every year. However, like other species of fish, particularly the sockeye, the returning numbers of the kokanee fish have decreased to almost nothing.

Government decisions to ransack, plunder, and pollute the land and water through mining, clear-cut logging, and other industries including sewage waste disposal destroy entire ecosystems. Despite the government and industry push for Indigenous people to rely on grocery stores and an economy-driven food industry, Indigenous communities continue to rely primarily on traditional food sources. Our primary grocery store remains the land and waterways: seasonal rounds of hunting, fishing, harvest of roots, plants, berries, and natural medicines. Denying Indigenous people the right to access and govern our traditional harvesting, hunting, and fishing grounds places Indigenous people in a state of continued poverty and starvation. It denies Indigenous families and children the right to nutritional health and well-being. Furthermore, it denies Indigenous people the right to successful participation in a contemporary economic world. The more things I learn about Canada and its lack of integrity in relationships with Indigenous people, the more frustrated I feel. There are so many multidimensional issues that continue to affect every element of our existence. Prior to leaving my community, I didn't understand the full spectrum of the impact industry and government had on our traditional food sources. I didn't understand the genocidal history of government policy with its discriminatory, colonial laws and all the multi-faceted ways they impacted our communities.

Post-secondary and my time living with and working for the Stó:lō have awakened me in ways that I am still learning to understand.

Prior to the draining of Sumas Lake and the redirection of all waterways within what is now Sardis, Chilliwack, and Abbotsford, the Stó:lō people could literally fish in their own backyard. They weren't starving. They weren't in poverty. They weren't fighting diseases; they were tremendously healthy and wealthy in ways relevant to sustaining vibrant Indigenous children and livelihoods. They lived in prosperity and their very life source was in copious abundance. The draining of Sumas Lake signified an epic and catastrophic change for the Stó:lō. Every spring, Sumas Lake grew to cover 44,000 acres with the spring freshet, extending from Chilliwack and Yarrow to Abbotsford and across the Sumas border into what is now referred to as the United States. Imagine all the species of fish, including all species of salmon and sturgeon, returning to find their home gone. Why were we never taught about the draining of the Sumas Lake in the public school system? How did the draining of Sumas Lake impact all those Elders and their descendants? The people went from being healthy and prosperous with an abundance of fish to being malnourished, poverty stricken, and devastated.

In the Halq'emeylem language, the word tomiyeqw translates as "great-great-great-great grandparents and great-great-great-great grandchildren." The translation of this word had me pondering many things, including the deeper dynamic translation that would not just be understood, but embodied, if spoken between fluent speakers of the original language. I can't count the times I have heard my Elders share the importance of abiding by these teachings of the past and future generations. People of the north, south, east, and west all abide by these. If we, as Indigenous people, had international laws, this would certainly be one. To honour ancestral Grandmothers and sacred Grandfathers of the past but also the livelihood of future generations yet unborn. To be cognizant and humbly aware of the resilience, courage, and strength of our ancestors in every aspect of daily life. To honour, monitor, and protect our traditional practices, languages, teachings, and territories, the waterways and all living things including the plants, for future generations. All to sustain an environment where future generations can thrive. This reflects the teachings of my Elders in the Nicola Valley as well as Indigenous teachings I've heard across tmíxʷ.

When the Elders came to visit at my godparents' house, the coffee pot and tea kettle would always be on. They would scoop a spoon of sugar into their cups of Red Rose tea or coffee, then stir. "Ting ting ting," their cups sang late into the night as they listened to one another and wove stories in Nsyílxcn, Nłeʔkepmxcín, and english. Spílaxm are the day-to-day stories, the remembered stories of things that were witnessed and events that took place. Men's hunting and fishing stories, women's stories and memories of living and working the land, cowboy stories, and stories of spiritual practices. These were happily told with pride. In my childhood, I had never heard anyone share sptékʷł in the traditional way, at bedtime. A book titled *Our Tellings* explained that these were the stories of a time when animal beings spoke and walked the land with humans. What I learned was that the sptékʷł say that the animal beings were the ones that taught human beings the laws of conduct, respect for all living things, and how to care for the land.

From *Our Tellings*, I learned that when my Elders were children, "stories, told repeatedly, taught them about nature, respect, morality, and proper behavior; they also served as a form of entertainment." These stories were orated at "gatherings, funerals, potlatches, hunting and fishing camps, root- and berry-gathering camps, and so on." Stories, mainly sptékʷł, were almost forgotten because for many years they weren't shared in the evenings, with the children, the way they once were. As a result, like myself, did not have the opportunity to learn them. What hurt the most was reading the words spoken by an Elder, "Ask by the graveyard, for when the elders die, they take with them an encyclopedia of knowledge."[1]

With the Elders, life stories and memories are deeply intertwined with the land. Many stories are of travelling great distances from the Nicola Valley, throughout British Columbia, and down into the United States, following the harvest of roots, food, medicinal plants, and berries. One of my favourite spíləxm is about my pregnant grand-auntie, when her baby came into the world after significant travel by horseback to the berry-picking grounds in our highest alpine mountains. Our people travelled through the Coquihalla Mountains, Boston Bar, Fraser Canyon, and the Nicola Valley, to the Okanagan Valley, to traditional berry-picking grounds, salmon-fishing sites, and village sites. Sometimes they shared stories of interactions with animals and spiritual experiences. Sometimes they shared stories about the Fraser River Gold Rush or the highway and railway construction through the Fraser Canyon and all the Chinese labourers that were brought to work in the Canyon. So many people died building the railway. Many

---

1 Darwin Hannah and Mamie Henry, eds., *Our Tellings: Interior Salish Stories of the Nlha7kápmx People* (Vancouver: UBC Press, 1996), 11.

of those deaths occurred for no other reason than those people, Indigenous and Chinese, were considered disposable.

Sometimes they reminisced about childhood memories of Indian Residential School and learning about agriculture and farming. Some days, they reminisced about bootlegging. As agriculture and fruit harvest became normalized, the people became fruit pickers. Indigenous fruit pickers often travelled for work throughout the Okanagan in order to harvest from fruit-bearing trees. Other times, Grandpa, his friends, and others reminisced about great big gatherings at the hop yards.

"What's hops, Grandpa?"

"A plant," he responded. This was followed by a long pause and then someone added, "Beer is made from hops."

"Beer is made from a plant? That's weird!" That was followed by the chuckle of Elders and further explanation.

"Every summer, people travelled from all over to harvest hops in the Fraser Valley. Same as when we all travelled to pick fruit in the Okanagan."

"I remember going to the Okanagan with my godparents when I was small. They would park in the shade of the cherry trees and let me sleep in the car while they picked." There was a moment of silent reflection throughout the room. I remember the front dash of the old truck and the windows left open when I woke on the seat of the truck. I would cry around, calling for my godmommy until I saw her legs descending a wooden ladder at a nearby fruit tree. The orchards were lined with tall grass and row upon row of trees, loaded with fruit. Through the years, we often travelled to the Okanagan for rodeos. On those trips, my goddaddy and godbrother would load the horses in the horse trailer. When we went for the fruit harvest, we didn't bring the horses. "At nighttime, I remember we slept in a little cabin. I'm guessing those were for the pickers." The Elders nodded in agreement.

"Yes, everyone travelled to pick fruit, at least until the Mexican folks started doing the harvest. After that, there wasn't any work left for us." I imagined a time when my Elders were children. Because of the anti-potlatch laws Native people weren't allowed to gather in large groups for any kind of event or cultural ceremony. Nor were they allowed to have organized meetings, yet one place they were allowed to gather in large groups was for the annual harvest of hops.

Queen Victoria's birthday on May 24th, 1865 marked the beginning of an annual day of waterfront celebrations at Victoria's harbour front. During the time when laws still prohibited Indigenous groups from gathering in large numbers, coastal Indigenous Nations began an annual tradition of travelling from as far north as Haida Gwaii, and south of the "us Border" for cedar dugout war canoe races. By 1867 the "May Day" birthday celebrations and canoe races were also being celebrated in New Westminster, BC. Stó:lō, Coast Salish, and West Coast ocean travel canoes began to change into the streamlined, extremely lightweight, and fast-turning, cedar race canoes. Through this process, cedar canoeing transformed from the daily uses of fishing and travel into a highly skilled and culturally disciplined Coast Salish traditional sport. Canoe racing is a sport that many Nations remain passionate about, right to this very day. The Syílx have many stories of travelling the interconnecting lakes throughout Syílx territory in cottonwood dugout canoes; however, I don't know these stories.

The first time I read my auntie Maria's book, *Halfbreed*, I was a kid. It woke up my mind, and gave me the understanding and courage to recognize the things in my life that weren't right, such as alcoholism and the violence perpetrated against women that I witnessed and experienced as a child. Later, in my teens and twenties, I began to put the pieces of the puzzle together. I gained a deeper understanding of the "why" of things. Why the Canadian government created Indian Residential Schools. Why our Elders were afraid to speak their language. Why for many years, our Elders didn't teach our parents and us younger generations our languages. Why my auntie would cover her mouth when she spoke our language. Why most of my family lived on reserves yet my mom and I weren't allowed to live on reserve. What it meant to be enfranchised, disenfranchised, non-status, status, or Métis.

My dad's family in Saskatchewan didn't live on reserve. I imagine Métis people as descending from wildflowers, wild strawberries, rolling prairies, jack pine forests abundant with wolves, deer, and waterfowl; woven with stories of traplines, fiddles, alcoholism, frustration, and the Red River Jig. Blood lineage, traced to the generations before contact, intertwined across tmíxʷ, Scotland, France. If there is such a thing as an original "Canadian" it is not the oppressive and racist european colonizers and settlers who set out to destroy everything about the original inhabitants of this land; it is the descendants of Indigenous women and the early fur traders or Hudson's Bay Factors. Métis people are not a random mixture of blood lineage that includes Indigenous and white european. The Métis are a very specific and distinct group of people in Canada who can trace their lineage to the intermarriages between Indigenous women and the original fur traders at the time of contact. Métis—vibrant with culture, fluid in their knowledge of the land—were denied the right to peacefully raise their children and harvest on the lands of their Grandmothers. Resulting in their road allowance homesteads. Small amounts of grasslands between the road and Crown land. Why? They were not Indian, nor were they white, so the Métis were not considered a people.

What does it mean to have multiple generations of children taken away for part or all of their childhoods, to Indian Residential School or into the foster care system? "Imagine a community without children." Imagine an entire country where every single Indigenous baby and child is taken away from their family. Imagine a country where every single child is raised in an environment where love, patience, compassion, and affection do not exist. Imagine a country where every single school has a graveyard and not a playground. In Canada, the theft of Indigenous children into foster care and mass "child apprehension" has resulted in generations of children lost and stolen from almost every single family in our entire community within the Nicola Valley. Generations of children stolen from every single Indigenous family across Canada.

The silence after the children were stolen must have thundered through our valley and all across what is now Canada. The silence must have haunted our Elders day and night. How could they sleep? How could they carry on? How did they survive such utter heartbreak and devastation, without the singing voices of their babies and children? Not knowing if their children were alive or dead. Did they have food? Who held them when they cried? Who could possibly comfort their broken hearts and childhood injuries? How many generations of our grandmothers and grandfathers feared for the safety and well-being of their stolen children?

I understood now, why so many Loved Ones remain heartbroken and angry. I understood why so many Loved Ones live in despair and struggle with addictions. When they stole all the babies and rounded up all the children, when they forced Indigenous people off their lands and onto reserves and road allowances, when they denied access to traditional fishing and hunting grounds—they shattered the hearts and spirits of our people.

The Elders have said that before european contact, the lights from everybody's fires lit the Fraser Canyon like northern lights across the sky. Hundreds of thousands of Indigenous people lived along the Fraser River right from the ocean entrance at what is now Musqueam, through the Lower Mainland, Fraser Valley, Fraser Canyon, and all the way up to the northern reaches of the Fraser River. The Fraser River and other major rivers traditionally did not just function as a river; they were major highways that provided our primary food source of all species of wild salmon for Indigenous people throughout British Columbia.

Stó:lō orator and historian, Naxaxalhts'i explains that the smallpox epidemic arrived in British Columbia and Western North America, long before european colonizers physically arrived here. George Vancouver arrived in the Pacific Northwest in 1792 and at that time, found villages that were completely decimated. We have heard many stories about the trade blankets, contaminated with highly infectious european diseases, that were "gifted" to Indigenous people in eastern North America by early traders in the 1700s. The Indigenous trade economy is vast, and as a result, the smallpox epidemic and then influenza travelled quickly. Oral traditions speak of smallpox travelling like a wave, hitting village after village along the Fraser River, all the way into Northern British Columbia, resulting in the tremendous death of Loved Ones. Our ancestors had never before experienced such complete devastation. Our

Elders tell us stories of entire families placed inside pit houses before the smoke hole and exits were sealed.

The constant sorrow that our people face within today's generation began during those epidemics, the dying years. When we were at our weakest, colonizing governments executed destructive policies, and Indian Residential Schools, with graveyards and not playgrounds, were developed for the purpose of solving "the Indian problem." Every single child was stolen from every single Indigenous community across Canada.

Anishinaabe oral traditions speak of North America as "Turtle Island." Despair fell upon Indigenous people all across Turtle Island like a great blanket covering the Turtle's back, woven of the same despair that devastated generations of our ancestors. And now the tattered remains of those blankets of sorrow need to be lifted and put away. As each generation courageously relearns cultural and spiritual practices and responsibilities, new blankets made of love, joy, healing, and perseverance need to be woven.

When I was a little girl, I used to hide under my godmom's kitchen table and listen to the Elders. I remember asking what this meant and what that meant. I was told by my godmother, "No more questions, Babygirl. Don't interrupt when your Elders are talking. When it is time, you will understand." The pieces are coming together now. Is this what "coming to my senses" means? I'm finally waking up. I'm awake to who I am, now. And finally, I understand what has occurred in our world as Indigenous people across Turtle Island. At the same time that I feel powerless, I also feel rage. I feel uncertainty. I am aware of the work we need to do in order to transform the despair. I want to help; I want to fix things and contribute to bringing joy back to the hearts of our people.

After work, I have nothing to do, nowhere to go, no one to hang out with. The road to Cultus Lake is foggy and mysterious. I imagine the ancient beings that once walked this land. Woven with the stories and songs of ancestral spirits. Stó:lō temexw is ancient like my home, ancient like Syílx temxulaxʷ, like Sḵwx̱wú7mesh temíxw. Ancient like Xʷməθkʷəy̓əm, or the traditional territories of the Tsilhqot'in, the Wit'suwit'en, and Nisg̱a'a; the Kwakwa̱ka'wakw, Nuxalkmc, and Haíɫzaqv. Ancient like Athapaskan and Dene ancestors who travelled all across the Turtle's back, from north to south to east to west. This place with its dark grey sky and endless rain is so close on the map, yet it is worlds apart from Scwéxmxuym̓xʷ.

During the summer, the temperature in Scwéxmxuym̓xʷ is so hot you can fry an egg on the sidewalk. Dust devils, sagebrush, and tumbleweeds trundle through town with the many gusts of wind. Yellow grass-covered hills gradually roll into pine- and juniper-covered mountains. Willows and cottonwood trees mark the waterways. Tmíxʷ is parched and covered by a spongy blanket of crispy, dry pine needles. Back home a tinder landscape is commonplace.

Fog and low clouds rest like a great blanket of mist around the hemlock and cedar trees across Stó:lō temexw, blurring the mountains. If not for the rain, Cultus Lake would be glass. I park and walk across the grass. It is a shade of green that doesn't happen in our semi-arid landscape back home. In the short walk from car to beach, I am drenched yet exhilarated by the sound of pouring rain drumming across the lake. This is not a landscape; this is a waterscape. Never in my life have I experienced such a continuous downpour that obscured absolutely everything. The lake monsters that our Elders talked about back home would love this kind of monsoon. I wait for a loon to sing but nothing comes.

Nicola Lake is at least twice the size of Cultus. The Elders say there's an underground river that joins the Okanagan Lake to Nicola Lake. The Ogopogo would travel back and forth between the two lakes. They said it often rested beneath the cliffs on either side of Nicola Lake before continuing through the channel beneath the mountains as it travelled to the Okanagan. I've heard our Elders say that many of the lakes throughout the Nicola Valley and Southern Interior are connected by the footprints of giants. However, I can't tell these stories because I do not carry this knowledge.

My godmom told me that every animal has songs—loons, grizzly bears, and porcupines are just a few. Some of their songs are medicine songs; some are calling songs. They all have a purpose but rarely does any person hear them sing. She shared stories about being a girl and travelling everywhere on horseback. One time, she had a nap under a tree up the hills by Fish Lake. When she woke up, a porcupine was in the tree above her. "Porcupines are really timid and shy," she said. "They are not fierce at all." When she woke, that porcupine was singing in the tree above her. I often wonder, when the wind blows hard across Nicola Lake, is that the Ogopogo singing? I often wonder about the Ogopogo, the ćuweneytmx, the little people, the cedar people. The mystical creatures and beings of our lands, where have they gone? All their secret sacred places are gone now. There has been so much development. The encroachment by people is overwhelming, and all the secret sacred places are besieged by the noise and destruction of people.

From the front steps of the concession, I watch as the coach from the canoe club arrives on the beach wearing a rain jacket and a wide-brimmed hat. He stands at the water's edge, looking out over the water. When he turns he squints at me in the Native way, as though trying to recognize me. I imagine his thoughts: Whose daughter is that one? Is she a niece? Is she a relative? I know he is looking, not at me but at the bones shaping my face. The mist rising off the water lingers in the air around him and rain pours off the brim of his hat. He turns away when he realizes—I am a stranger—then walks up the beach and out of sight.

I sit in the rain, listen as voices multiply and echo across the water. I told my friend that I would be here. I didn't say that I would walk over to their camp, intrude. Instead I listen to the music of their presence and watch as they carry their canoes to the water, then stand knee deep, unaffected by the April chill. Finally, one by one, eleven men get into one canoe, and then ten women with a skipper climb into another. That is when the canoes come alive. They follow one another, paddles simultaneously reaching, digging, until their canoes disappear into the mist and rain. They leave only their wake and their voices calling switches. I feel as though I have witnessed the ancients at the water's edge, but for them it is an ordinary day.

snow on the mountains

he
stands at
water's edge,
gazes over the water.
mist lingers in the air around him
as rain pours off the brim of his hat.
one hundred years earlier he would have worn cedar.

on
the beach
we are merely
sisters and brothers
learning from one another
an ancient kind of strength.

soft
and rolling
his words reach
a place deep within.
his laugh is as peaceful as his face.

he
says:
you are only
as strong as your mind.

mist
on the
mountains.   snowflakes
and hail dance with the rain. the sky is dark grey. somewhere in our world the frogs are singing.
we gather here each day, embrace our paddles, blade up—handle resting in pebbles and sand.
the lake is a blanket of glass beneath the rain—a rush of sound as it falls. saturated: tmíxw,
hemlock and cedar trees, houses, sand, stones, grass, the dock, canoe pullers standing
on the beach, children playing nearby. perhaps we could be home, warm and dry.

Salish Dancer

blue sky collects on our skin, thick and warm.
today, the leaves do not dance,
the birds and the squirrels do not sing.

in the distance, ripples of a hungry fish
unfold in lazy circles,
around and around and around.

coach and bow-lady wait at the picnic table,
encircled by a bouquet of douglas fir and hemlock trees.
one by one, men, women and children gather,
their voices and laughter are respite from the day.

they are golden in the sunshine:
Little Zim, 50/50, Lil' Five
Mountain Breeze and *Salish Dancer.*
great cedar beings, they rest
on canoe racks nearby.

"men on the *Breeze.*
women on the *Dancer.*"

the ripples begin
when the canoes touch water
the trees begin to dance minutes later.

we paddle away knowing our coaches watch:
each switch, each slide, each stroke.
not one paddle is out of time.

Stó:lō temexw.
lined with houses, residents oblivious
these canoes have travelled here
warmed these beaches
for thousands of years.

white caps swiftly congregate as we paddle.
when we reach the middle the winds meet us there,
howling over the mountains,
heavy with dark clouds, mist, and rain.

lightning mushrooms across the sky
and moments later, loud and pounding,
the world sings.

waves, all foam, up and over our heads,
waist-deep, mindful of our coach's teachings.

"it doesn't matter how rough the water is,
stay focused.
don't let fear take over
and never stop paddling.
remember, cedar never sinks."

we paddle until skipper hollers,
"everyone, jump out.
we have to roll her over and bail.
whatever you do, don't let go
and don't lose your paddles."

rising and rolling with the waves
we hold tight to the *Salish Dancer* and tread water
until the *Mountain Breeze* sweeps through the mist.

unafraid, the men jump into the water,
amidst storm and waves.
together we rock the *Salish Dancer* hard, side-to-side
to get the water out then climb back in again
then skipper hollers, "Header home!"

we arrive wearing mismatched flip-flops,
eyes wide, laughing and some crying,
men on the women's canoe,
women on the men's canoe.

on the beach coach stands unsurprised and squinting,
"looks like you all went for a swim."

our paddles in hand, we move as one across the water,
the strength of temexw surrounding us.
together we paddle her song,
together we paddle her dance,
the beautiful *Salish Dancer*.

The Kingfisher's Dance

I'm bleeding profusely…somewhere. I know I am. The sky is blue; the sky is so, so blue.

"READY!" our skipper hollers; his call echoes across the lake.

"One, two," ten voices answer. Before finishing "two" we switch and slide and continue paddling on the other side of the canoe. My co-worker's sister sits ahead of me. She slides her paddle into the water, pulling as white foam swirls around her blade. I follow suit, keeping time with her stroke. My ass is raw in two patches where tailbone connects to cedar. Cedar bum has no discrimination and all of us have it. I fumble, lose my grip, and make a sloppy stroke.

"Stay in time!" Skipper calls.

At least it wasn't in the middle of a switch! Like a lawyer, my friend argued her case in a daily negotiation process. She listed out my daily activities, or my inactivity to be more precise. "It's the only traditional sport in all of British Columbia." I admired her forearms and shoulders, beautifully sculpted. I've always wanted that kind of strength. And she was always so disgustingly happy: smiling and laughing every single morning. I had to give in. When I started, they called me "Wrists all the way up" because my arms were so skinny.

I am sitting in a cedar dugout canoe. Who am I trying to fool? I don't belong. I'm not strong enough. Lift then reach and spear the blade into the water. It's clockwork. It's a drumbeat. No looking around, not at the birds, not at the water, and definitely not at the jumping fish. Maybe if I just paddle lightly.

"Pick it up!" Skipper calls. Half an hour earlier, we were pushing a tire for resistance. Reach, dip, pull back, reach, dip, pull back. The muscles in my belly, across my back, in my arms, shoulders, neck, the muscles in my legs and across my feet are all fully engaged. The rhythm of eleven blades lifting and dipping into the water keeps me going. *I. Can't. Quit.*

I want to eat strawberries. Ripe, red field strawberries.

Cultus Lake is a brilliant, emerald green. *Salish Dancer* is the name of the women's canoe. She is golden in the sunshine and glimmers with every stroke. Yellow cedar reflecting sunlight, submerged and glistening in the water. Cedar in my hands, cedar beneath me, cedar all around me. If pain could be medicine, it is this pain, here on this water in this canoe. *I am choosing this pain the same way I am choosing this water.*

Pain, wash over me; cleanse this heart with your presence. Show this body what it feels like to be strong. Teach me to endure and learn the strength of our Salish ancestors. Teach my spirit to sustain when all else wants to fail.

Eleven blades in the water, reaching and pulling, reaching and pulling. Eleven voices call switches as the kingfishers glide over our heads. A solitary eagle observes from the cedar, fir, and hemlock trees on shore. Our lungs are infused by the breeze as it flows down the mountains and off the lake. The only thing that exists is cedar, water, the sky, and all of us, here together.

In the distance, I do not see stones along the water's edge. I do not see white foam along random waves, nor do I watch the kingfishers as they dip and dance along the tips of waves. I do not listen when the eagle's song echoes from beach to beach. I follow my canoe sister's stroke and quiet my weakened mind. Sadness, sickness, sorrow. Let everything go with every stroke. Carry nothing back to shore. *Your only job right now is to breathe, pray, and paddle.*

Reach. Dip. Pull back. Reach. Dip. Pull back. At the end of the lake I pray with every muscle, cell, and fibre of my being.

"ONE BOWMAN!" Skipper calls when we reach the buoy. Our bow-lady buries her blade hard for the turn and everyone digs deep with their paddles as the canoe turns on a dime. "Pick it up, ladies! Let's header home!" The canoe is alive with our combined power. Paddles lift, muscles bunch then dig as each blade is buried in the foam left by our canoe sister's blade.

PB and J sammich and fresh red strawberries, here I come.

race day

waves gather and crash on the beach in front of us.
like a cooking pot, the water boils
thick and green with seaweed and kelp.

our team sits next to our canoe,
minds clear, we wait to race.

people congregate on lawn chairs, driftwood, and logs,
along the pebble beach, eating
barbecued sockeye salmon, potato salad,
fresh clam chowder and crab legs.

"women's eleven on deck!" the announcer calls.
we grab our paddles and one by one, climb in.
strokes sits one, two, three, i sit seventh,
Skipper is always number eleven.

a warm-up lap then paddle to the start line.
eight, nine, ten cedar canoes dance side by side,
lined up ready to race.

back up, move forward, steady in the rolling waves,
wind blows, minds focus, paddles raise,
salt crystals form on our skin.

"BANG" the start gun blows.
"GO!" Skipper screams, "HIT IT!"

eleven paddles slice the water in a sprint.
water boils behind each blade.
"READY!" he calls.
"one, TWO" we answer, switch then slide.

big canoes all around, we hit it again,
with each stroke our canoe lifts.

"REACH IT OUT! POWER!" Skipper screams.
immediately, our bow-lady reaches with
long, power strokes and we each do the same.

there's a tickle in my nose.
the hay fever kind of tickle.
the tickle is like an itch, with a need to sneeze.
i ignore it but the tickle grows.

we hear the glide of the canoe as it cuts through the waves,
the gentle dip and stroke, dip and stroke of eleven blades
before our competition paddles up alongside us.

side by side the gap between canoes disappears
and my rival, my canoe sister is by my side.
we growl, we snort, elbows raised,
blades tap tap tap with every stroke.

approaching the buoy, we pull ahead,
"who rea-day?" their skipper hollers,
"one, two!" and paddles hit water hard.

paddle hits shoulder, nip of blade across hand
and snot long and golden sways from my nose
as the crowd cheers from the beach.

"POWER!" Skipper screams.
the finish line is close,
the buoy dances on the waves.
i can taste the salt.

huh-up ~ WHO! huh-up ~ WHO!

simultaneous we all reach our blades and he screams,
"DIG DEEP! POWER!" and the snot sways.
do they see it from the beach?

if i had a Kleenex and a tentacle
growing out of my shoulder,
i might wipe my nose but
i'd probably use it for another paddle.

if i could spare a moment of concentration
i would lift my shoulder to wipe it
but i will not lift a finger from my blade.

the crowd on the beach is no longer sitting,
they scream, "Let's go *Five Star*!"
"give it all you got *Rainbow*, push it!"
"goooo *Geronimo!*"
"let's go *Stahloooo!*"

water bubbles and foams beneath our blades.
all power we reach and dig,
a drumbeat for our canoe and
she sings with each wave.

seat by seat we pull ahead
until we cross the finish line
champions.

quw'utsun

like a woven cedar hat, the wide brim shades
curve of cheekbone, lips, and chin,
sunshine hot pebbles and sand
gather beneath our feet.

cars, canoes, and pullers
line the road all the way to the beach.
skin tanned dark from relentless sun,
muscles defined by hard training.

i watch you walk with paddle in hand:
a paddler in your prime, an Elder within,
too far away to call, each step a dance.

season after season i find you
in the distance it is your form, the tilt of your arm,
blade lifted, elbow raised, grip gentle yet strong
until the start gun blows.

"BANG" paddles hit water,
nec'e, ísalaʔ, switch then slide
across cedar, smooth through the waves.

season after season you find me
walking along the beach,
standing by the concession,
at the start line.

sometimes you share stories,
or you share teachings.
at race time you remind me,
keep a clear mind.

sitting on the beach in the shade of the canoe
that rests upon the log i lean against.
with teammates nearby i am surrounded
by the hum of laughter and conversation.

i hear the rumble and bass of your voice
before i see your face.

sunshine, it reflects off of each grain of sand,
each crystal of ocean salt.

we find relief in the shade
until it is time to race again.

sorrow

September 16, 1998, 10:15 PM
Journal Entry

This is my second year of the Native Indian Teacher Education
Program (NITEP). I started with the college prep courses at the
Fraser Valley College in Chilliwack in order to upgrade for the
NITEP prerequisites. After I finally finished, I transferred from the
NITEP field centre in Chilliwack to the UBC campus.

Native Housing in South Surrey was closer to UBC than Chilliwack.
I don't know the city at all. Even with a map, the highway exits on
Highway 99 to campus don't make sense. I get lost while trying
to get unlost only to get lost all over again. On campus I get lost
trying to find my classes. And then I get lost driving home and it's
scary because that's at night and I'm alone.

Will this get better?

Walking through campus is like walking through a riptide of students; it's hard not to get caught in the surge. When I was a kid
and my mom was doing her teaching degree, Suzie and I would
always catch the city bus. It was much easier to remember which
bus to catch because we had two choices, "DOWNTOWN" if we were
going to downtown Granville Street or the "#10 to UBC" if we were
returning to campus.

I travelled to Vancouver to attend a "coffeehouse" at the UBC First Nations House of Learning in the Sty-Wet-Tan Great Hall. Coffeehouse is a weird name for an event. Basically, a coffeehouse is an event for people to share their performance, musical, or poetic talent. Seeing so many Native writers, storytellers, and musicians perform was super inspiring. And wow, the UBC Longhouse is amazing! Humongous cedar house posts with the walls all cedar. There's a huge student lounge with couches and a computer lab. "Home away from home." Indigenous students appear completely relaxed and at home. There was even a guy sleeping with his books in a big stack beside him and a book across his chest. People tend to call the First Nations House of Learning either "The UBC Longhouse" or "the longhouse." I keep wondering and waiting for the next coffeehouse but aside from the Welcome Back BBQ, I haven't seen or heard anything.

So far, my favourite place is the student lounge in the longhouse. I've made a few friends. Everything is different on campus. A lot of the Native students have communities and huge families back home. Others grew up in the city or moved from other provinces in Canada to attend UBC. Some folks are really friendly and love to laugh around and tell crazy stories, others are basically stoic. For the most part, everyone in the longhouse is pretty great. I haven't met anyone on campus that I'm even vaguely attracted to. And, I'm completely okay with that.

deer stew

Rolling along the Similkameen Highway, there is no better way to wake up than watching the changing landscape ascend to rocky peaks that rise to greet the sun. I know this day will be one blessed by blue sky. Young, single, female, no babies, a bit of courage, and a valid driver's licence mean my get-up-and-go is steered by the seat of my pants. I love travelling and this time my destination includes a visit with my beloved Elders in Chopaka.

My earliest memories of the Similkameen Valley are of waking up alone on the bench seat in the old blue truck, the air fragrant with morning mist and cherry, peach, apricot, or apple trees. Calf-like, I have memories of bleating my baby songs calling for my god-mom: "I'm awake now! Mommy! Mommy, where are you?" I would sit peering, sometimes through tears, out the open truck windows at tall grass and trees thick with leaves and heavy with fruit, search-ing. Soon enough I would see my godmom's bottom half, balanced on a ladder, her head in the trees picking fruit. She would care-fully descend the tree and comfort me with fruit fresh off the tree.

The Okanagan was a dot-to-dot drive as we explored thrift stores in search of treasures. We visited Loved Ones and travelled to rodeos in Princeton, Keremeos, Chopaka, Osoyoos, Oliver, and Penticton. The Omak Stampede and Prince's Department Store in Oroville, Washington were always highlights on our Okanagan Highway adventures. We drove with the windows rolled down, the hot Okanagan wind blowing through the cab of the truck. One of my goddaddy's arms tanned dark while he sipped on a glass bottle of Coca-Cola.

During the winter months, road trips to the Similkameen were for sacred Okanagan winter ceremonies, sn'ix'wam. Also called the Medicine Dance. The Cathedral Lakes Powwow is also nestled within the stunning Similkameen Mountains, and today that is my destination. With windows open wide and the air conditioning turned off, I hear the drums several minutes before I pull into the powwow grounds.

The heady scent of sage and pine hits me full-on when I park my car. The air vibrates with the awesome sound of bells and whistles and drummers singing to the heartbeat of the land. A multitude of vibrations: children running dusty from non-stop play, crying and laughing and the twang of the MC's orator voice, rich with an accent that signifies his identity as representative of a Nation far from the Similkameen. The songs echo high into the rocky crags and alpine meadows, all the way up to the clouds so that even the ancestors must be dancing.

"Sister!" It sounds familiar but maybe not because there are lots of sisters here today. That's when I see my sínciʔ. "Hi Sister!" He waves and smiles. I walk over, shaking my head.

"My sínciʔ! Your voice changed! I almost didn't recognize you!" He and his dad, my stepdad, are sitting at a picnic table eating warm deer stew and fresh, hot fry bread. "Where's our seester?"

"She's looking at crafts with Brenda." Brenda is my stepdad's new wife. He parted ways with our mom years before and instead of losing a dad, we gained another mom. My brother's deep man/boy voice throws me off, and I'm shaking my head listening to him.

"It wasn't that long ago since I last saw you, was it, Sínciʔ?" I thought only a few months had passed? "C'mon, give me a hug! I missed you!" He stands up and my jaw hits the ground. Ostrich-like, my baby brother towers above me, and when we hug, my head rests on his shoulder. He laughs and gives me a noogie. For the first time ever, I feel small beside my baby brother and I am astounded. That's when his dad laughs his deep and gentle laugh.

"What the heck happened? You were shorter than me just a few months ago! Sínci?, you must be almost six feet tall!" He'd only turned fourteen just a couple of weeks earlier. He wasn't that tall during his hockey tournament in February, was he? That was the last time I'd seen him. Well, he was mostly on the ice that weekend, and every time I saw him, he was geared up. I can't stop staring at him, so I look at his deer stew instead. My heart is swollen with pride and his dinner smells amazing. My tummy growls. "Mmmm, don't go anywhere; I'm going to grab me a bowl of that!"

When I come back from the concession, his dad is gone, looking at the arts-and-crafts vendors. My brother and I choose a seat in the stands. When our sister joins us, we all share a bag of red licorice. The lady dancers are so graceful their feet barely touch the arbour dance floor. We walk around and around the outer and then the inner circle of the arbour, looking at vendors, visiting friends and Loved Ones. My brother's and sister's friends, boys and girls, come and sit with us and walk with us for a few moments, enjoying the energy of the powwow as nightfall approaches. It's only a matter of time until they ask.

"Do you wanna go walk around?"

For the first time ever, my sínci? responds, "Naah, I'm gonna hang out with my sister for a while." I feel so proud to be an older sister. It feels so good to sit with the two of them in the stands, my brother so handsome and my sister so beautiful. I blinked and missed it, their lives. And suddenly they are no longer babies. Suddenly they are grown teenagers.

I was the kind of sister who wasn't always around. Almost thirteen years older and away at university, I was focused on my own life—that of my twenties. I missed a lot of the events that were important to both of them. As they got older and I came home to visit, they began to act cool. The last time I saw my brother was at the hockey arena; he waved in that cool teenager way, "Hey Sister."

"Don't 'hey Sister' me, give me a hug!"

"Sister, no!" he said, with his face bright red.

"Don't be cheap, Sínci?. Can I have a hug, please?"

"Sister!" His buddies stood around laughing. I hugged my brother hard, doing the choo-choo train as he tried walking away, the way only I could. Oh, how I loved to torment him.

"But Sínci?, I haven't seen you in so long."

"God, Sister, why do you do that?" He was laughing. I knew he was embarrassed but I was so happy to see him. His friends stood nearby; most I had known since they were children having sleepovers at our house.

Hockey team after hockey team, small hockey skates grew, hockey gloves and pads, and a great, big, smelly hockey bag and an endless photo of you, my sínci?, with your arms spread wide, running across the rugby field, surrounded by teammates, receiving the biggest wedgie I'd ever seen, having just scored a goal with a rugby team that I never once saw.

Looking back, I've wondered what I would have said or done differently if I had known it was going to be the last time I ever sat beside my brother, heard his voice, and marveled at how much he had changed. Since they were babies, they had never called me by my given name. They always referred to me as "Sister," regardless of who was around, regardless of where we were. That comforts me. My brother had grown so tall; his chest had become so broad. A young man, confident with his sports, confident among his friends, an honourable young man who stood up for the smaller boys at school.

If I'd known what was ahead, I would have put myself in his place. I would have begged the Creator not to take him. But instead, we walked around the arbour, ate deer stew, fry bread, and red licorice, drank juice, laughing, teasing, and talking. And when we said our goodbyes, it was him, disappearing into the crowd with his friends, waving, smiling, and telling me, "I'll come back to see you before I go, Sister. I promise." It was them leaving the powwow without saying goodbye, not knowing, and me sitting in the stands watching the dancers dance, waiting for that goodbye.

i dreamt of you last night

my sínciʔ
in every stage of life.

at every age
at every height
you ran
through my dreams
stopping only to wrap your arms
around my neck.

i love you, Sister.
you say over and over

i lift and swing you
around and around
for the whole world to see.

i love you too, my sínciʔ.
and then
you run away again.

in the dream

our tears
filled the lake
until the valley
disappeared.

landslide
mud
tears
and
memories
rocked
our
house
down

with
ropes
nets
and
bloody
hands

i tried to save us all

tracks

high alpine mountains,
shale rock falls,
Similkameen Valley,
clear night sky,
full moon.

i am
alone
on the highway
at midnight.

i search

for your tracks

in the dust,

in the shadow

of the sagebrush.

i wait

in vain

for your next breath,

to hear

your voice

on the breeze.

little brown

                    in
                    my
                 mind's eye
          little brown little bear
          my brown bear brother you run
                through trees through labrador bushes fragrantly scented
                   coating your brown bear coat my brother clear as day you
                      rest your body across my lap your head on my shoulder heart
                      beating breath warm your hand in my hand little bear little brown
                      my brother you run through a field of tall grass stand on the
                      rolling hills of our home little brother with gentle forgiving
                      eyes little brother with gentle forgiving hands little brother
                        who wouldn't eat when you were s'posed to eat little
                         brother little   brown little bear
                         my brother!   please tell me
                         where do   you make
                         your   home?

September 24, 1998
Journal Entry

There's a place inside me that is filled with shame. I know it's there and it talks to me every damn day. It tells me that I am an imposter and a wannabe. Who am I trying to fool by attempting this university thing? I'm not smart, nor am I clever enough to achieve anything aside from failure. Why am I here? Why did I even bother? This is the chorus line inside my mind and sometimes I tell it to shut the hell up. But no matter how often I send it away, it always comes back again. The brain is just a muscle and its job is to think, but the recycled crappy thoughts are incredibly annoying.

I have to be honest. I'm grieving. I'm really REALLY GRIEVING! I grieved hard, when my grandpa died. I missed him so much, but he was an Elder. And his health had deteriorated so much, he wasn't himself. He couldn't enjoy living anymore. I had so many dreams of him on the other side, like, in the spirit world. And he was always happy in my dreams. I had no choice but to honour his decision; it was his time. But losing my brother! What the fuck, Creator? WHY? This doesn't make any sense! Sometimes, some days, I can't stop crying. And I can't move. I can't eat. I can't sleep for days. I can't believe my brother is gone. I can't believe he's gone. I have no idea how to fix what is broken. I don't understand why my brother died and why I'm alive. It should have been me.

There are random phone calls from friends. Sometimes, they come stay on my couch, so that I'm not alone. I appreciate that. A lot of my friends have disappeared. There's a guy. To be honest, he's mixed up too. I know life has shattered him. Too often, it feels like I'm being used for my vulnerability, and I'm tired of it. He lies about everything, and he thinks I don't know. But the important thing is he's a voice on the phone and when he calls, he's the only one courageous enough to fish me out of my deep, dark holes. I don't make excuses for him, but I don't expect anything other than accepting him where he is at in his healing journey.

I've started reading Louise Hay. I've decided, I can heal my life too. One day at a time, one breath at a time, one moment at a time. One teardrop at a time. I can do this, I know I can. I've started seeing a counsellor at the UBC Longhouse, on campus. It's a lot of work retraining my brain because the negative ninnies in my head always jump in, right when I least expect them. It is lonely, but I've learned that I feel safest living alone. I've created my safe place, my woman cave. One of my strategies is writing positive affirmations on notes and sticking them everywhere: bedroom, bathroom, kitchen, and even my front door. A lot of them are direct quotes from Louise Hay's book as well as other books and prayers. Another thing I've been doing is like an internal challenge. Every time I catch a negative thought, I balance it out with a positive affirmation. So I try to catch myself before the spiral starts.

I know I'm not a genius. I came to university even though I have failed many times in elementary and high school. I'm terrified. I love creative writing and I love to read. I love our Indigenous languages too and took entry-level courses in several. Since I've been attending UBC, I've been taking Xʷməθkʷəy'əm language classes at the Musqueam Elders Centre. Xʷməθkʷəy'əm is the actual word for "Musqueam." Musqueam is a badly anglicized pronunciation. I found a basement suite on the Musqueam Indian Reserve and rented it. It costs more than the place in Native housing out in Surrey, but I'm five minutes away from campus now and I feel better.

October 1, 1999, 10:15 PM
Journal Entry

I'm scared. Not of a person or a place or any "thing" in particular. I'm scared of writing things down and sending my words out into the world. It's like what our Elders tell us, "Be careful of the words you say because once they are out in the world you can't take them back. Our words have power." So, what I say here is only for me and you and no one else. There's a brokenness inside of me that hasn't healed and I don't know if it ever will. But I'm trying. Creator, I'm really trying to carry on.

What I've realized at university is there are so many Indigenous students here, all far away from home. All of us are from different communities, representing different Nations, yet there is still not enough of us to transform our world. That's why I'm writing this. It's a letter home. It's a letter to Indigenous youth. A letter to our Indigenous communities. And I'm saying we need to stay alive. We need to continue the work our Elders and ancestors fought so hard for. Through starvation. Through the loss of their children, land and through all their tears. And now, we have to do our healing work and persevere. We can't give up. I'm writing this in the privacy of my journal but this is my prayer. It's highly unlikely I could ever publish this. Maybe the creative writing courses I'm taking will help me set my voice free.

Sometimes I feel like I could be at residential school too, a contemporary one. Far away from home for so many years, immersed in city culture and lifestyle. Before I left home, I was catching on to our language, but now I've forgotten a lot. I was spending time with my Elders, learning, and gathering traditional foods and medicines. I was doing a lot of community stuff. Now at university, everything is different and part of me feels as though I am forgetting who I am. So I am writing this to remember.

I was raised Nłeʔkepmx and Syílx, in the Nicola Valley, British Columbia. Although I didn't know what it meant to be Nłeʔkepmx and Syílx, Interior Salish until, gosh, quite possibly when I moved in with my sk̓ʷóz.

Living on the Musqueam Rez feels safer somehow, safer than the rest of the city because people know one another here. It feels good. Even though it's not my community, it is a community. And even though I don't have aunties here, someone does, and knowing that is comforting. When people see me, they smile and say hello. And that's nice too.

I'm lonely for the smell of the land back home. Waking up to fresh, dry-cold morning air, almost sharp on the skin. When the sun is rising, and mist is hanging off of every blade of grass and every branch on the trees. And the grass fields roll into hills. And the hills roll into mountains covered with pine and stone. The sun reflects on the moisture and lights everything up. That's what home is: it's alive.

In Musqueam, I wake up each morning and it's different. It has an ocean-fresh morning smell. The difference is the moist, humid ocean air. On the mornings when it's not raining you can smell the rain in the air, especially in April. On the mornings when it is raining, there is either a torrential downpour or continuous drizzle and the sky is perpetually grey. Except I try not to taste it because of the air pollution.

I'm supposed to be working on homework, but I can't concentrate so I've started writing in this journal.

Coming to university is all about dreaming. dreaming to create something. to heal maybe? to achieve transformation. maybe a better life...

With Each Stroke of My Paddle

He's gone, for real he's gone, my baby brother. And everywhere I go, I am a shadow tied to tmíxʷ by a string. I want to cut this string and free myself. May 23 turned into June, our canoes were put away because they are in sorrow too. The beach where we gather for practice is deserted and the lake is silent without our voices calling switches. Sometimes I go there just to sit. Pace back and forth at the water's edge, watch the ladies on their pink canoe, and listen to the music of their laughter as they paddle out across the lake. July turns into August. I don't want to give up or take time off from university.

My truth: I didn't enter the NITEP program because I wanted to be an elementary schoolteacher. What I really wanted was to be a writer and that goal seemed silly. Seven of my aunties as well as my mom's closest friends all got their teaching degrees through NITEP. Teaching seemed to be the most logical direction, but I had to pass all my required and elective courses for the Bachelor of Education program. This included Math 335 and History of First Nations in Canada.

History of First Nations in Canada. Whose story is it anyways? And who has the right to say how those stories are told? Six credits in Canadian history to fulfill the Bachelor of Education graduation requirements. The course starts in September and finishes in April. I absolutely refused to take a general course in Canadian history because I knew it would just feed me the same horseshit I was force-fed all through elementary and high school. I wasn't about to have my head pumped full of a history that didn't engage the truth, the embedded, rooted, and deeply suppressed history of Indigenous people here in Canada. History of First Nations in Canada began with standing room only; however, by November, classroom attendance had dropped so that over three-quarters of the desks were empty. Maybe because of midterm stress. Maybe because it was another long, dark, rainy winter.

The history of First Nations peoples is, apparently, an uncomfortable subject to teach. Our instructor's classroom behaviour is erratic. Her behaviour indicates that she is not fond of Indigenous students voicing their perspectives in the classroom. Seeing as the whole course is about us, shouldn't we be allowed to express our insight and experience? Many of us quote from the lived memories that our Elders shared with us. Years of sitting silently through slanted, incomplete, and, ridiculously false interpretations have become tiresome. One particular evening, her lecture, with the overhead slide presentation, turned into a verbatim repetition of the previous week's lecture. Several students packed up and walked out of the classroom. The comments ensued, "Didn't she show these slides last week?"

The following week, a private meeting with her in her office regarding a paper led to her enraged voice echoing throughout the building, into the stairwell two floors down, following me as I left the building. History of First Nations in Canada transitioned into a directed study. By late January the history department had received so many complaints that they removed her.

By February and March, my godmom was in and out of the Kelowna cancer clinic. My young mom and I weren't talking, again. How could I understand her sorrow when I could not understand my own? In her darkest days following the loss of my brother, how could she possibly light up for me when I could not even light up for myself? A head-on collision with an elderly man who ran a stop sign ended my semester early. Life was overwhelming. With a medical extension, I submitted a 20-page final paper and failed the History of First Nations in Canada. Failing in the telling of our story was most certainly an epic fail. I failed all of my courses except writing for children, a two hundred level creative writing course. A year had passed so quickly. It was already springtime and another semester was complete.

—

By carrying on and returning to university, was I thinking that I could forget the fact that everything in our world had shattered? Pretend that my baby brother was still alive? Sorrow is cunning. Sorrow is baffling. Sorrow is powerful. Sorrow is an all-encompassing thick, heavy fog. It is a blanket that covers the world. It blinds vision, smothers daylight, and within its darkness my body is an empty shell. The world is dark even on the few sunny days.

I am planning it a hundred different ways. I'll drive into the lake. I'll drive off the cliff. I'll cut my wrists. I'll find pills and OD. I'll jump off the bridge. I. Am. So. Tired. Of being alone. Of living. There are a few friends who have stood by, who have been brave enough to withstand this storm. It's hard to constantly reach out. Instead, I sink into the silent darkness of my mind. And then my cellphone rings.

"Nic?" Her beloved voice on the other end calls me back.

"Yeah." I don't know what to say. She's caught me at a bad time. I'm so happy to hear her voice. Tears gather and roll down my cheeks. She becomes my kite string even though she doesn't know it.

"I'm just calling to schedule an interview." I forgot that I had sent in my resume.

The lawns on the Coqualeetza grounds are bright green, fresh with the scent of rain and springtime. The office has moved for the third time, and this time, it's in a beautiful new building. There's a new receptionist. The previous office was a tiny heritage house located on the Coqualeetza grounds. Prior to that, they were located in building #5, which at one time was the Coqualeetza Hospital nurses' residence. I worked across the hall from them when I was a transcriber for the Aboriginal Rights and Title Department. My office at that time was an old janitor closet. Anxiety rolls around inside my stomach over all the potential ways I could fail. Maybe I was too happy, too friendly, laughed around too much?

When my name is called for the panel interview, I am squirming in my seat. I sit on my hands in order to focus. The interview is at the back of the building, in the manager's office.

"Can you describe your previous experience coordinating youth programs? Do you have experience with event and program coordination or management?" There are several individuals participating in this interview panel, a program officer, a representative from the board, and the manager. The manager is also chief of one of the local Stó:lō communities. His hair is greying, and he has a beard. His eyes are not brown nor are they blue; they are piercing yet kind. I did a short-term contract helping this department with the organization of the annual Stó:lō golf tournament. I remember him. I know that when he smiles, his entire face lights up. He has daughters; I remember because he had such pride when he spoke of them.

"Yes, I've had a number of coordinator positions: coordinator for summer camp as well as language and cultural programs. I was a volunteer coordinator for student-led events at the UBC Longhouse. I also assisted with coordinating conferences, a few golf tournaments, and the 1996 BC Elders Gathering." As a boss, he was always easygoing, friendly. He would often talk about ways he wanted to positively transform the future for Indigenous youth, and it was always through employment, skills development, and self-empowerment.

"I want to tell you about the training opportunity that this position will focus on. My goal is to create and implement a pilot employment and training skills development project for teams of youth that will run on a weekly cycle for eight weeks. Each week, my hope is that youth will gain employable skills and employment certifications. This is important because in the long term, the skills they gain will provide them with confidence, motivation, and open more doors for career opportunities." The photos scrolling through his computer when it's on sleep mode say he's a horse guy. I like horse people. There are more questions, specific questions about management and coordination skills, forms, overseeing and working with organizations. The position is a training position for a post-secondary student, so I qualify. They will call after they have completed the rest of the interviews. If I get the job, I will have to move back to Stó:lō territory.

When they call back, the answer is yay! I pick up boxes from the local grocery story on West 41st and Dunbar and pack up my basement suite. I'm so happy and inspired that my canoe pulling muscles suddenly awaken.

The best thing? I can paddle away the sorrow.

She'd forgotten the kettle on the stove while I was at work, my tiny little Syílx godmom with her auburn hair in braids. It boiled until it stunk and the metal was stuck to the element. When I got home from work at Stó:lō Nation, I pried the kettle off the stove and then bought an electric kettle with an automatic shut-off feature. She stayed for two weeks. She even came to Cultus Lake for canoe practice. She was so small; she looked like a child in my passenger seat and sat on two pillows in order to see the road. She followed me around my house, dried the dishes that I washed, held the dustpan as I swept. She didn't say much but always stood nearby, watching. I guess she knew the heaviness that was in my chest. She'd experienced it so many times throughout her life.

Sorrow. If anyone knew sorrow, she did. The only way I found out was when we visited one of my Elders in Kamloops. My beautiful Syílx godmom sat at the Arborite kitchen table with my beautiful Secwepmx Elder. Two cups of steaming hot Red Rose tea sat nearby and they spoke the way Elders do. They quickly realized that they had both attended the Kamloops Indian Residential School at around the same time and reflected on shared memories. Where they slept. Where they ate. Things that occurred while they stayed there. "Do you remember that girl they whipped with the electrical cord?"

"Ohh yes. They took her away. There was so much blood." I was shocked and silent. Cigarette smoke rolled in slow circles above them as they sipped their tea. There was a balance between silent reflection and quiet voices. Family photos hung from every wall and a framed glass picture of jesus on a cross rested under the window, on an antique sewing machine. These were stories that I had never been privy to. The stories heard as a child growing up were always day-to-day stories that involved jovial teasing and jesting, stories about the animals, those who came to visit, who was sick, and local community news. They never ever spoke about residential school.

"I was so scared."

My hands were restless, turning the lighter over and over as I listened. Once again, I tucked my hands under legs and sat silent on the chair between them. Enraged, powerless, and silently hurting. Hurting for their lost childhood. Hurting for everything they witnessed and experienced and the love they didn't receive when they were so small. This was the first time I had ever heard her speak of that place.

"They never brought her back. I always wondered what happened." These words weren't jovial. They weren't in jest. They were the words shared in the silent hours between Elders and my body was grieving. Our dear Secwepmx friend had her long hair rolled into a bun. She paused to light a new cigarette; inhaling then exhaling, as smoke rolled in the air above them. My tiny godmom had her long auburn hair pulled back in an auburn braid, her blue eye blindly reflecting a childhood scrubbing hallways. They paused in silent remembrance.

My godmom would rarely speak Nsyílxcn out loud. But when she cried, Nsyílxcn was all she understood. I was in the bedroom at my birth mom's house when my younger brother passed, overwhelmed by the singing, deep mourning that grows and grows until tendon, muscle, bone, and heart are torn from chest. The kind of sorrow where the spirit stands apart, watching, helpless to ease the pain. Singing out crystal tears that represented every single moment shared and unshared with each of our Loved Ones who have gone before us: my sínciʔ, Grandpa, my godmother. Memories are like blades of grass, like flower petals on an alpine meadow covered by wildflowers, pluming, unfolding, leaves reaching. Memories are multi-faceted crystal drops of rain falling from the sky, landing on each perfect petal. Brother, our brother, how could you possibly be gone? My sínciʔ, please just come home.

Kitchen, living room, dining room, outside around the fire, our Loved Ones gathered: cooking, cleaning, telling stories, singing, praying, chopping wood, and taking care of our family. The people had been gathering since the word went out to the community. There were so many children and youth at the house, they were everywhere, inside, outside, running around in the darkness even though they weren't supposed to do that at a péɬec. The purpose of a wake is for Loved Ones to gather in honour of the one who left us and to support the grieving family. The spirits are awake, the door is open to the spirit world, and children are not supposed to run around at night. But the question was profound and overwhelming among everyone who gathered: how do you ease the hearts of children, their teachers, their parents?

Night, sunrise, dinner, afternoon, the hours rolled into one another until the third night came. She cried with me, her wails echoed throughout the house. When my godmom cried, I always came to her side, but this time my spirit was shattered. I couldn't breathe. I couldn't speak. Then like an older sister, an Elder that she loved came and spoke to her, almost sharply, in Nsyílxcn. After that, she gathered herself and sat silently holding my hand until I was okay. Those Nsyílxcn words were what she needed to wake herself. Sometimes, I wish I knew what our dear Elder had said.

One day as I folded laundry, my godmom spoke to me with pride layering her voice. "Babygirl, you were listening."

"I…what? When?"

"When I taught you how to take care of things, to help others. When I taught you how to clean, how to work. I said move fast with your hands. Don't be lazy. Never stand around trying to be cute. At gatherings, at péłec when the people gather, when you're visiting; if there's work to be done, get up and do it. No complaining. Your job in life is to help the people. I've been watching the way you do things, how you work. I see that you have listened to my words." I didn't know what to say; warmth filled me and my eyes watered. I continued taking clothes out of the dryer. Listening and folding as she spoke.

On the day she returned to Quilchena, I drove her to the bus depot and stood watching her board. She was so tiny, already so frail. I was afraid for her safety. Tears poured down my face when the bus pulled out of the parking lot towards the highway, carrying her away. I wanted to chase the bus, stop it, beg her to stay. Later that night she called to tell me she was home. She said that she had cried too. She said she had wanted to ask the bus driver to let her off again.

Put everything into training. Allow the water, the wind, rain, hail, tmíxʷ to do the work. Tmíxʷ will fix it, tmíxʷ will lift it, tmíxʷ will wash it away. I made a decision to set my heart free. Sorrow doesn't ever really leave; the memories never wash away. I made a deal with the Creator: Turn the suffering into strength. Sometimes I silently cried with each stroke of my paddle, tears mixing with sweat and rain. It was a relief not to think.

I am on a different canoe, a beautiful pink canoe. The ladies are so strong, and our coach is kind. His words are full of love and guidance. I am grateful to sit and paddle with them. To make their canoe sing. In unison, I follow my new canoe sister's blade with my own. We have all been touched by this, by grief. We have each lost Loved Ones. Recovering from loss takes time. We learn to live with it; we learn when and how to put it away. We wrap it up and place it in a cedar tree. Put it in the water, let the river wash it away. Train our minds to pray with each breath, pray with each stroke. Pray for those members of our families left behind.

yémit and merímstn

Teapot Hill

I look at the trail as it disappears into the bushes. I know where it goes. I take a big drink from my enormous water bottle, cap it, and throw the bottle back in the car. No cellphone, no water bottle. Too bulky to carry. No bouncy pockets, car key tied to shoelace—I am ready to run. I need to run, to let go, to stop carrying the past. I took time off from university to work through my grief. Working in Stó:lō temexw and running mountain trails. One day I would like to hike Mount Cheam and Elk Mountain. But right now, I'm too scared to go alone. For peace of mind, I focus on the easily accessible trails that are frequented by other women.

July: sun shining bright, clear blue sky. Straight up the mountain I lumber with a slow, consistent pace: walk-jog through the steepest parts until the trail levels out, rising and falling alongside cedars and ferns, moss blanketing the trees, stumps, and ground. This path is a cathedral. Is it the day or is it the place? Despite the pain in my back, my body feels strong. My footsteps feel like drumbeats. I pick up speed. Running along the winding trail, cresting hills, jumping mud puddles along the smooth black soil all the way to the top. For so many years, I lived trapped within my pain, carrying my hurt like a blanket of stones that weighed heavy on my heart, mind, body, and spirit. I didn't know how to breathe. Everywhere I went, I always held my breath: on the canoe, while running. I realized that holding my breath is a behaviour left over from childhood trauma. Holding the breath creates anxiety; it causes a struggle within the body to live. And so, learning to breathe deeply and regularly has become a big part of my healing journey. Allowing myself to breathe meant allowing myself to live. Training on the land and water, running, paddling, cycling, and hiking taught me to have endurance. This training taught me to push through the pain until I found my strength.

The rhythm of footsteps along dirt trails has become fluid with dreamtime. With every footfall, running from valley to valley, from the ancient ancestral sptékʷł , the time of talking animals, transforming into the future, into spiləxm and present-day life stories. I never feel alone. Along my peripheral view there are always ancestors nearby: beside me, inside me, all around me. The process of transformation is fluid, is constant. Running and walking mountain trails helps my release. Even on rainy days, there is tremendous peace to be found among the trees, their great branches reaching for the sky. Whether the rain is falling like ribbons from the sky or the sun is glinting and reflecting a thousand lights off of each leaf, fern, and bush. The moss, brilliant green and full of life, hangs in great draping blankets off the branches of trees, blanketing even the many stone faces of the mountain. In the distance, tiny speedboats pull water skiers across the lake. My eyes follow the water's edge around Cultus Lake, observing each of our canoe training points of destination: the army base, first point, second point, until we reach the end of the lake.

There is a beaver house there, in a small bay at the end. Early one morning a beaver was following my canoe as I paddled, until it suddenly slapped its tail on the water and dove deep within. On another morning when I was out on my single, a mother deer stood on shore, silently watching me as her tiny newborn fawn stood on awkward legs nearby. The lake has become my home, the mountains a place of healing. There are lichen designs along the cliffs where wild tiger lilies grow, in a secret spot along the rocks. Every spring, I wait for those tiger lilies to bloom.

After reaching the summit I return, running a good pace along the rolling black soil. My pace builds until the only thing that feels natural is a sprint. The trail turns to mud and then to rocks and sharp-edged stones. Soft black earth and cedar trees with thick, ancient moss beckon. I am no longer running. I am no longer here. I am breathing. I am flying where the spirits dance at the tops of the trees. The trees fan one another, gracing each other with songs and stories, their gentle hands raised to the sky. Inspired by the beauty of the day, by the strength of a growing, healing heart and mind. Breathe, breathe, breathe, daylight, sunshine. I listen to the drumbeats in my chest until my foot makes contact with one of the many sharp-edged stones.

I am a bird. I am a plane. I am a cannonball.

I fly, roll, and slide along the gravel until my crumpled body stops. Dazed, groaning on the ground, I roll onto my side and try to stand. Excruciating pain shoots lightning strikes up and down my leg. I hobble and drag my body close to a minuscule stream. If I were an ant, the stream would be a river. Thirsty, I am so thirsty. I consider putting my tongue there and lapping water.

Deeply grooved, my knee holds the mountain: stones, dirt, gravel, and a hunk of bloody flesh hang. *tmíxᵂ, spirit, human, road-kill.* I laugh to myself even though the situation is not funny at all. Is that bone I see embedded with gravel? I lift the bloody flesh: body and brain scream. Hand to knee, pressure on the pain. Dizzy, thirsty, dirty, bleeding along the path—how lovely. Inspired, what the hell was I thinking? Who daydreams and sprints down mountains without water?

Foreign voices spin in and out, if only I could hold my head up. I am so sleepy. Two Asian men speaking unrecognizable words walk towards me. "Okay? Okay?"

"No, no…not really." They are a blur as they continue their jaunt downhill. Their voices fade. Rolling in and out of fantasies of healing in time to do the upcoming mini-triathlon for first-timers, I fixate on that tiny stream alongside the trail. If only I could just lap at that rivulet of water.

"Do you need help? Are you okay?" I lift my head in a woozy, drunken way. A man and a woman are walking the path together. Bloody and embarrassed, I answer.

"I think so," I slur, and give my head a shake. "I'm thirsty."

"Honey, did you bring your first aid kit? I think she's in shock. We brought this extra bottle of water. Drink this." She hands me the water. My hands fumble, clumsy and thick. She takes the bottle back and opens it for me and hands it back. "What happened?"

Pride is absolutely useless. I am thankful for the pure brilliance gliding down my throat. The cool water brings back my awareness. "I tripped."

"Can you stand?"

"I tried but my knee. I have the mountain in there." Their eyes seek to appraise my injury, but my hand is covering it.

"Here, hold onto my arm. If we help you stand, do you think you can make it to the bottom?" The man grabs me on my left side and throws my arm over his shoulder. They are so friendly, but then, hikers are almost always smiling.

"I'm not sure." His wife reaches around my waist and they hoist me up. The weight on my leg is too intense.

"I need to secure that chunk of flesh because it falls open when I stand. The pain is unbearable. Do you want to see?" I lift my hand off the gaping maw that is my knee.

"Oh my goodness. Is it broken? Honey, are you sure we don't have anything?" He digs around in his waist pouch. He kneels and looks the wound over.

"I'm trying to figure out if that white stuff is bone or tendon. I don't think it's broken." Sitting on the ground again, I pull off my shoe and sock.

"Can you bend your knee?"

"A tiny bit. I can't put weight on it."

"Okay, I see. We don't have any Band-Aids." I consider everything on my body for possibilities. Car key tied to my shoelace; I am empty-handed. Aside from my socks I do not have anything. I am not the wisest trail runner.

"My sock, but it won't stay in place."

"Well the good news is, you wouldn't be able to move if it was broken." He pauses and appraises the situation. Then he looks in his gunny sack again. "Why not try tying your sock to your knee with your shoelace?"

"Ohhh!" I immediately pull my shoelace out of my running shoe and secure my sock across my gaping, bloody knee. The relief is instant, and we are on our way. Other hikers and runners pass by, trying not to stare at my injury as we make our way to the bottom. "Thank goodness for people with big hearts." Waves of exhaustion flush over me. As we approach the trailhead, two paramedics walk up the trail from the parking lot.

"I gather that you're the injured young lady we received the call about?"

"Ahh, yes, I probably am."

"Okay, we can take her from here." They instantly hoist me up off my feet and carry me down the remaining trail.

"So, ah, am I right to assume I am riding in the ambulance?"

"Yes. How else would you get home?" I never realized paramedics were so friendly. "What were you doing up there anyway?" I really don't want to tell them.

"How did you fall?" One paramedic holds me as the other quickly pulls out the gurney.

"A gurney? For real?"

"Are you well enough to stand and walk?" The throbbing pain sends waves of dizziness at the thought of standing.

"I was running."

"You were running the trail?"

"Yeah. It was great, until I tripped."

"Sounds like an excellent run. My son and I should do that. We usually run the Rotary trail." Surprised, I lie back on the sterile, white pillow. Then the paramedic pulls out a huge, long needle.

"What is that?" I ask, surprised by the size of the needle.

"Morphine." The ambulance is idling, and the amount of medical machinery in it is impressive.

"Yes, it's a great run. Just—" Nausea threatens and my throat closes as he squirts clear liquid in a clear arc from the tip of the needle. I close my eyes, talking non-stop until the needle pierces flesh, "—don't daydream when you run Teapot. Okay? Especially down that straight stretch. It feels good but just don't daydream. Do you think I'll heal in time to do the mini-triathlon?"

"Guaranteed you won't." Then he scrubbed the mountain out of my knee.

This process of healing is endless. It is within. It is a healing of mind as well as spirit. It is a healing of layers, of generations. Of grandmothers and grandfathers, of mothers and fathers and brothers and sisters. Healing is a lifestyle. Setbacks don't mean failure, it is time to pause, to reflect, and to realign. Time to reassess and re-envision. Courageous acts of healing and resurgence require the endurance of our ancestors.

this trail

alive with sound
mist enshrouded
cedars

blessed by the waking of day
blessed by the birds overhead
blessed by the sunshine
blessed by the rain
blessed by the breeze

seeking something stronger
transforming what is broken

run through hurt
run through sorrow
run to stop thoughts of suicide
run until my feet lift

amidst ancients,
arms outspread
join the Creator

blessed by the waking of day
blessed by the birds overhead
blessed by the sunshine
blessed by the rain
blessed by the breeze I create

unceded

we gather amidst cedar house posts
floors of cement and stone,
this is our home
away from home.

on unceded Xʷməθkʷəy̓əm traditional territory
we represent our Nations
at the First Nations House of Learning,
University of British Columbia.

At home on our traditional homelands,
our relations span generations:
cousins aunties uncles grandfathers grandmothers.
this longhouse roots us, heals us.

as we mend ourselves
we mend one another.

studying staying focused
our purpose is strategic

manifest healing transformation

we are the future generations.

Huckleberries Are My Weakness

I am an urban hunter-gatherer and I am shopping at Capers, an organic grocery store in Vancouver's West End. I step silently from ceramic tile to ceramic tile looking for the organic muesli with the most dried berries. I settle for blueberry-almond. From the cereal aisle I venture onward, searching for fresh, new greens. In a moment of contemplation, I remember one of the most important teachings I ever received from my Elders, that of balancing the traditional Indigenous lifestyle in which I was raised with the convenient lifestyle of the dominant society.

I grew up in a small town in the Southern Interior of British Columbia. I am proud to say that on my maternal side, I am of Nłeʔkepmx and Syílx ancestry. During the winter, I went to a public elementary school, unlike my mother's and grandparent's generations who attended Indian Residential School. During the summer months, my entire family would pack up tents and coolers, and travel great distances to gather traditional food. In the spring, we gathered wild celery, wild rhubarb, wild potatoes, bitterroot, and tree sap. When the wild rose bushes bloomed, we knew the sockeye would soon be filling the rivers, and my family would travel to the Fraser River to fish with traditional dip nets. Later in the summer, we gathered saskatoon berries, chokecherries, soap berries, then travelled to the highest mountains to gather black huckleberries. My cousins and I would pile blankets into the box of the truck and lie there for the duration of the trip, telling stories and giggling until we fell asleep.

Amidst trees, bushes, and grasses that grew higher than our heads, my cousins and I would gather wildflowers, Indian paintbrush, glowing bright red and orange; unsuccessfully we would tug on tall, brilliantly pink fireweed. Then, crawling through the grass, we would wonder and fantasize about the fairies that wore the lady slippers.

Surrounded by loud infectious laughter and the gentle rhythm of the language spoken by my Elders, I sat near my mother with a pail tied around my waist and gathered handfuls of shiny, black huckleberries. "Ting, ting, ting," they fell into my bucket, rolling around, taunting me with their sweetness. But my ever-watchful mother would say, "Don't eat the berries that are filling your bucket!" Tart, tangy, and sweet, the berries were irresistible, so I would stuff handful after handful into my mouth every time her back was turned. Afterwards, I would have the telltale signs: purple lips, purple tongue, purple cheeks, fingers, and palms.

During the winter months, the hunter-gatherer became the midnight-freezer-raider. Slowly, bag by bag, my mother's precious winter preserves of huckleberries would diminish, savoured by my thievish mouth. Her voice hollering, "Nicola, where are my huckleberries?" echoes through my mind as clearly as it echoed through the house the day she discovered her precious pancake rations were gone. Today, that phrase reverberates back to me with a dozen different meanings. Where have my huckleberries gone? Or better yet, what have they become?

I am standing by the purple grapes in the Capers produce section. I bite into a grape and sweet juices flood my senses. I hate buying bland grapes; they have to be sweet and tasty before they receive any appreciation. My friend professed to me her great love for frozen grapes. Her senses have not been intoxicated by the overwhelming melody of flavour found in ice cold, sweet and tangy black huckleberries; not the red huckleberries that so many West Coasters are fond of, black huckleberries. That's when I know: I am not only a hunter and gatherer of food, I am a hunter and gatherer of life experiences.

My first love was raised like me. The two of us would spend endless days in the mountains, driving or hiking. At home we would have the senseless arguments that young people have, and, in the mountains, we resolved them. In the spring, we gathered fresh, new greens. In the summer, we helped his mother and aunties preserve sockeye salmon and berries. In the fall, we went hunting for deer and moose. In the winter, we went ice fishing. But of course, things change. We moved to the city for his education. When all the jars of salmon were gone and there were no more huckleberries to be found, I realized that I needed to allow myself to grow and to dream. I began my journey of hunting and gathering alone.

In cedar dugout canoes, with wind, rain, and hail blowing in my face, I hoped to gather the strength and discipline of my ancestors. My Elders said balance is necessary to survive.

Standing on the beach in the pouring rain, I taught my canoe sisters the "looking-for-a-good-man dance." Laughing, we envisioned situations where we could practise our hunting, catch-and-release strategies. But Indigenous men are hunter-gatherers as well. Late one night I realized this when one sang Indian love songs to me from out on the street. My theory was affirmed again when I discovered I was one of many—like berries in a bucket—girlfriends of my new love. While listening to the radio, my newest flame said he thought notching his guitar to mark his passionate endeavours was wrong: His guitar was far too precious. Then he professed my perfection, his insignificance, and said the timing was off and went east in pursuit of his goals. He was a hunter-gatherer too.

I came to the conclusion that it was time to pursue my gathering elsewhere: gathering life and work experiences, gathering dreams and goals. Now I am doing things that I never would have experienced had I stayed at home in the Nicola Valley. At university, I further my education. On the water, I participate in traditional cedar canoe racing—a Coast Salish traditional sport that is not practised in my home territory. I work out at the gym becoming physically fit; becoming aware of my health and nutrition. I have my own home, which is my safe place. My car transports me anywhere from the northern tip of Vancouver Island, to the University of British Columbia, to my home in Chilliwack, to my home in the Nicola Valley, and to my auntie's home in Batoche, Saskatchewan. I have accumulated memories of love, loss, and grief; clothing that never seems to stay in style; a stereo; and of course, music. Someone somewhere said those things are important. At university, I gather knowledge: a + b = c. I never made it through math, but I learned the gift of the spoken and written word, and of course, academic discourse.

Where is the balance between academic education and traditional education? Where is the balance between the city filled with pavement, tall buildings, and smog and the mountains, filled with the sweet, enveloping scent of pine, fir boughs, and Labrador tea? In a place where my existence is as clear as the intricate patterns on the sidewalk beneath my feet, it would be so easy to become confused about my identity. The city becomes more real than the community where I grew up. And the valley of my childhood remains more real than this city filled with cement, buildings, and millions of people.

Back at Capers, I remember the shock of an early morning bath in ice-cold mountain water while refilling my recyclable water bottle. With sudden overwhelming clarity, I realize that real balance between traditional and contemporary, bad and good, new and old, exists nowhere else but inside.

medicine song

amidst this miasma of buildings and people
pavement highways
pollution

books stacked high
crumpled paper on the floor
words falling off the page,
row after row
final exams and final papers
are due.

public education my frustration
edged by historic untruths
colonial education colonial expectations

Old Mom all i want
is to come home to you.

i can run
i can paddle
leave campus at midnight

you said "stay"
until my assignments are complete
chocolate-covered espresso beans on hand
wide awake with caffeine

and i hear your voice singing
    hey ya heyyy…
    hey ya heyyy…
    ho…

across the Coquihalla Mountains
on the cold winter breeze,
through the Milky Way

moonlit sky, fresh snow falling
lonely high mountain highway
sagebrush, cottonwood trees, rolling terrain

my home
is calling me

your medicine song
is calling me
home.

pressure canner rhythms

one eye blue as a midsummer Quilchena sky,
one eye brown as the trunk of a ponderosa pine.
hair in ringlets or in a single braid,
she's an Okanagan cowgirl.
Fish Lake flows through her veins.

she is my beacon i am her tumbleweed
rolling searching learning
this harvest season i bring my gathering.
a cooler full of sockeye.

clean, debone, fillet, stuff jar after jar.
scales glitter across countertops and hands
half-pint mason jars line the counters
pink with sockeye, vinegar, salt.

walker nearby, she wipes rims clean
watching the flick of my wrist
tightening lids.

sanitize counters, cupboards, floors.
there is comfort in shared presence

steam rock rock rocking
shake, shake, shaking
loading unloading reloading

pressure canner rhythms in the night.

sx̣ʷúsm

the hours when all you hear is the sounds of floorboards creaking,
old house shifting, settling into night.
synkẏép yaps echo across the hillside
winter moon high in the sky.
no snow on the ground.

silent and introspective she draws her puff,
clouds of swirling smoke rise and circle
until she suddenly snuffs out her cigarette
and rises from the couch, reaching for her walker.

slippers swish swish swish as tires roll,
unclipped chihuahua claws clickity clack
along the tile floor.

into the kitchen they go,
cupboard doors open,
old wooden drawers close
and then the clink of metal and glass.

that's when curiosity pulls me
to follow her swish-swish to the kitchen.

"only a glass bowl works" she says, "only use a glass bowl."
she places a quarter teaspoon of bright red berries and juice
swishes & rubs it inside of the bowl, then rinses it out.

"prepare the surface by removing any oil" she says.
"if there's residue on the surface, it won't foam."

she crushes red berries with a spoon.
adds a bit of water, sugar waits on the counter,
then her brand-new electric hand blender
drowns out the noises of night.

red crushed berries rise into pink foam.
sprinkle sugar sprinkle sugar sprinkle sugar
until the pink foam becomes
stiff glistening peaks.

———

the first bitter spoonful of sx̌ʷúsm savoured
in the heart of winter,
tmíxʷ blanketed and sleeping

becomes a journey to the place of memories
where our Elders who are gone, now live.
the berries red like lifeblood emerging from
ancestral Grandmothers' birthing water.

to be Syílx
to be Nłeʔkepmx
to be of this tmíxʷ this glorious temxulaxʷ

travel snow-blown highways
from north south east west
navigate mountain passes
on the prayers of Loved Ones.

Syílx longhouse.
we enter this sacred circle after the sun has set
shake hands, acknowledge each person
seated on benches and chairs, smiling.

gentle laughter and quiet joy
heartbeat drumbeat in this place
of winter songs,
winter footsteps dance upon tmíxʷ
until roots awaken and grow.

bountiful, blessed sacred foods
sx̌ʷúsm spíƛ̓m síya c̓əlc̓ále smíycuy sqyéytn
the roots, the berries, the four-legged, the ones that swim

all around the circle,
we feed the spirits of ancestors,
there they are, they sit,
among us.

—

the moment when the first bitter yet sweet spoonful touches our lips
we return to those sacred places inside ourselves
where our ancestral child spirit is,
the place of our Grandmothers and Grandfathers.

this is why we pray
remember
give thanks
have giveaway.

when the work is done
we put everything away, we must go
our separate ways. we must let them go
again.

Spring Chicken

I turn off the highway and follow the road through the Quilchena Indian Reserve. A cloud of dust follows me as I turn onto the dirt road leading to my godmom's house. My car rattles past the old CMHC houses, deserted shacks, tractors, the old rodeo grounds, the horses, and Rosie, the mountain goat who was adopted by the herd of horses. Finally rounding the last curve, I park in my godmom's yard. I was born the same year she lost two children in a house fire. She was a first cousin to my grandmother. She started babysitting me after we moved home from the prairies. I am not certain how old I was when I was baptized and she became my godmother. She loved me as her daughter. In a time post-Indian Residential Schools when countless generations of families were picking up pieces and surviving through post-traumatic stress, we became medicine for one another.

When I open my car door, I can already hear the dogs barking and the television blaring. I knock and open the front door. The heat from the wood stove takes my breath away. Noopy, Tina, Lady, and Tiny—her dogs from my childhood—fill my memories. They are gone now. Rocky and Coco, her Chihuahuas, instantly jump on my legs. She's sitting on the couch across from the doorway, facing the TV. She looks up surprised, cigarette mid-puff. She snuffs it out and turns down the television. "Babygirl!" Her smile lights up the room.

"Hi, Mom!" I kick off my shoes, sit beside her, and hug her. "Whatcha watchin'?" Her waist-length hair, normally auburn, is abnormally dark. That means one thing: the hairdresser accidentally dyed it too dark. Definitely a sore spot for her. And it is tied back in a dishevelled ponytail.

"Oh, just the news." She has lost weight again. She'd always been small, but now she is maybe seventy-five pounds. She looks even more pale with her extra dark hair. She had turned seventy-one in April. Tiny and strong, an old-school Syílx cowgirl.

Bible Bill, the bootlegger, shot her from his roof when she was in her twenties, when the prohibition made it illegal to sell alcohol to Indians. "I bought groceries one day and we had all this fresh meat in the refrigerator. I brought the kids to town, and when we got back the meat was thrown all over the kitchen. The police went in and found him upstairs. They made me identify him. He was half crazy. Bible Bill, he shot me with his .22. Anytime someone asks me how I lost the sight in my eye, I always say, 'It was for alcohol.' The doctors were afraid that if they removed the bullet, it would kill me. They put a steel plate right here in my temple, and that's what holds that bullet in place." Ever since then, her one eye has remained pale blue like the sky.

"Did you eat yet?"

"I'm not hungry, Babygirl." She's reaching for her cigarettes. I disappear into the kitchen before she finishes her sentence. Flicking on the light, I open and close the cupboard doors, then grab her rice pot, fill it, and put it on the stove. This is our routine whenever I come to visit. I cook her dinner, and we sit together late into the night. She smokes and reflects. She is Mom, I am Babygirl. I try not to pay too much attention to her extra dark hair because I know well enough that she is feeling self-conscious. It's hard to imagine a time when she would have had short hair as a little girl at Indian Residential School. She was always so particular about taking care of her hair. Gathering fallen strands from the floor, gathering fallen strands from the counters and off her combs. And, like my Syílx Elder from the Similkameen, she shared very specific teachings about how I should take care of my hair. Always pick it up and take care of it. Don't throw it in the garbage, don't flush it down the toilet. Put it away in swift moving water; bring it to the mountains. Don't bury your hair because that is a sacred part of your being and your power.

"Mom, where's the salmon I canned for you?"

"Oh, it's in the kitchen somewhere."

"No, it's not. Is it in the back room?" I push open the door to her spare/laundry/storage room, full of clothes, bags of flour, sugar, cans of coffee, soup, toilet paper, dishes, dolls, and stuffed toys that she still buys for me. I found all of the jarred salmon under the bed, four unopened cases of canned fish. The extra small 125 mL jars were the perfect size for one meal. Looking at the jars, I realize the problem is that she can't open them. I grab a case and put it on the kitchen counter.

As I cook, she sets up her makeshift baseball field for her Chihuahuas in the living room. I have no clue how she trained them to play baseball, but it's the funniest thing in the world. It makes her happy and thoroughly entertains both her and her dogs. She sets Coco in one corner, Rocky in another corner, hits that ball, and explains to them their bases. Oh, there's so much excitement to their game. She starts hollering and the dogs are barking. Rocky and Coco chase their ball from base to base until they win their game.

"Mom, your hair is all messy. Can I comb it?"

"You be careful! Don't pull too hard, that hurts, and don't braid it too high. That hairdo isn't for old ladies." We move into the kitchen, so she can sit on a chair and smoke while I cook rice for our late-night salmon dinner. Standing behind her, I begin to carefully comb the ends. "That hairdresser dyed my hair too dark."

"I'll say!" She is embarrassed. I can tell by her tiny shoulders and her facial expression. In my childhood memories, she often has her long hair in rollers. Searching through her lipsticks, taking time to take care of her beauty and appearance. I have never risen to the same standard of self-acceptance for my beauty. I have always had shame for my appearance. She always had such pride in her appearance, especially when she fixed herself up. "Mom. Why haven't you eaten the salmon that I canned for you?"

"I haven't been feeling good, Babygirl." She puffs on a cigarette and then puts it out in an ashtray full of stubs.

"Mom, you need to eat. When I didn't can enough for you, you were upset with me. Now I canned extra and you haven't been eating. Your body can't get strong if you don't eat."

"They are supposed to bring me some Boost that will get me better." Gently, I slide the comb along each wiry strand. Her hair is smooth in my hands.

"Boost isn't food. You need protein. Please eat the salmon. Get Brother to help you open the jars."

"Babygirl, I've been talking to Danny about when I die. Only Danny and Beth and you know how I want things done." Nausea creeps into my throat and anxiety goes down my spine.

"Mom, what will you do when I die?" I pick up the comb, and prepare to braid. I've never asked that question before.

"Babygirl, I am going to die before you."

"You don't know that for sure. I could die tomorrow, my sínciʔ taught me that." A lump forms in my throat.

"I would cry and cry and cry, then I would die too." She sits with her hands in her lap.

"What if it wasn't your time?"

"I would die from sadness."

"But what if my spirit came and said, 'Mom, it's not your time to leave this earth. Your Loved Ones here still need you. Your work isn't finished.'"

She sits in silence then, her hands clasped in her lap, thinking about the Creator. She loves the Creator, God, Jesus, the Holy Spirit, Mary, and the bible. She prays every day, morning, night, over dinner, over her children and grandchildren, her pets. "Then I would be very sad, but I would have to keep on living. I would have to carry on."

"Mom?" I pause and wait for her to respond. I feel ridges along her scalp as I slide my fingers through to pick up the last piece of hair.

"Yes?" Her hair slips through my fingers.

"I love you, you know."

"I love you too, Babygirl." I finish the braid and wrap the elastic around and around the last few strands. It rests flat all the way down her back, not as thick as it used to be.

I lean forward and put my arms around her. "No Mom, I really, really love you. I love you with all of my heart: Nám ʔesx̌ʷəzcín skíxzeʔ."

"I love you with all of my heart too, Babygirl." After that, we sit at the table for late-night fish and rice. She even has China Lily Soy Sauce.

—

It wasn't the first time they had visited her. They had come many times before. Usually they entered through the back door, but sometimes they used the front door. Always in the middle of the night, always when she was sleeping, and always they'd ask, "Are you ready to come home?" Usually, it was her Uncle Adam who came.

She always said, "No. I still have lots of work to do," or, "My son still needs me."

The last time I was with her at her house, she was beyond frail; she'd lost even more weight. Her bones were angular and fragile beneath her skin. She was recovering from pneumonia, and before that a fractured hip, and before that a broken femur, and before that cancer, and before that, and before that, and before that. And me, I was the whirlwind that blew through her door. Her tumbleweed rolling through much too fast, the screen door screeching behind me each time it closed. She was sitting in her usual spot on her couch, and she lit up with joy. "Babygirl!" One of the last times we spoke was on my birthday. I called her and the phone rang a few times. When she answered, we chatted until I said, "Mom, guess what?"

"What?" Her voice sounded distant and tired on the phone.

"It's my birthday today. I'm another year older." She was silent for a moment.

"Do you have a boyfriend yet?" It was my turn to be silent and a bit confused. Why was she so concerned anyway? I didn't understand.

"Well, no. I wasn't looking." Gawd, why did she have to ask.

"Damn you, Babygirl! What are you waiting for? You're getting too old to be alone." Shock. I was silent. I didn't know what to say. She hadn't lectured me for years.

"Mom, geez. I'm okay. I don't need a relationship." But she was mad. She was really mad and she stayed mad—hang up the phone mad. Scratching my head, confused, I wasn't sure what to say after that. When I got to her house, I still felt a little bit nervous.

"Mom!" I hugged her, careful not to break her. "Gee whiz, I missed you."

"I missed you too, Babygirl." She was smiling with her eyes and I was sitting next to her holding her hand and rolling the loose, yellow skin between my fingers. She pinched me, hard.

"Ouch! Mom!"

"Tight!" She laughed out loud. "My skin was like that once, tight and smooth." Then she squeezed my bicep. "I had bigger muscles than yours."

"What?" I stood up and flexed my canoe-pulling arms and back muscles for her, striking a pose. "Your muscles couldn't have been bigger than these pythons! No way!"

"I rode horses every day and packed water all the way from the crick. I threw bales all summer. I went to cow camp and cooked in the kitchen. I was stronger than some of those cowboys!"

"Must've been lots of cowboys around back then, eh!" I smiled and winked.

"Ahh! You and your cowboys!"

"You and your cowboys!" And then she told me of their most recent visit.

She'd been wide awake, watching TV when the kitchen door opened. She'd looked over and her Uncle Adam was standing there, wearing his cowboy hat, chaps, boots, a scarf, and riding gloves.

"Ready to go?" he'd asked. She told me in english, but he'd spoken Nsyílxcn.

"No, not yet. I have too much to do," she'd responded.

Not yet. She was so frail; it hurt to look at her. I wanted to lift her up, take her into my arms, and rock her like a baby. I wanted my hands to be warm with medicine so that I could put them on her and take her pain away, make her tummy hungry again. I wanted to help her, to make her happy, to fix her somehow so that she could be whole and strong again.

With her words still fresh in my mind, I cooked like I always did, banging around in her little government house like a hurricane. Sweeping and mopping floors. Doing dishes and tidying. Pulling out her rice pot, counting jars of salmon—how many had she eaten? How much longer would she talk of the spirit world? She needed to talk of the spirit world. She took moments to remember everyone who was gone. She hadn't spoken about it as much in the past; now it seemed like she spoke of it every day. It had to be scary to leave. It was scary for me to accept. I was young and selfish. I was always leaving, going to town, going to Kamloops, the movies, going to the Okanagan, going all the way back to Vancouver on a snowy, stormy highway. Always on the go, going anywhere but sitting, waiting, watching, and listening to the spirits each time they came.

I was sitting in class at UBC in Vancouver when my cellphone rang. I had forgotten to turn the ringer off. Looking at the display, I picked it up and ran out of class into the hallway. My sister-in-law, my godbrother's wife, sounded distant and hollow.

"Hello?"

"Nicky?"

"What's happening?" It was unusual for her to call. She never calls, never ever.

"Mom's in the hospital." There was bile in my throat and it was rising. I was standing in the middle of the hallway in Buchanan B in the faculty of arts. Mid-semester, and students were everywhere, some with their backs against lockers, textbooks spread open across the floor in front of them as they did their homework.

"What's happening?"

"It's her heart, they can't slow it down. They don't think she's going to make it."

Rush hour and traffic was barely moving. It rained all the way to Hope, the base of the mountains. It rained so hard that I couldn't see, or maybe it was me. I don't remember the Bear Tunnel. I don't remember the snowy highway. I parked outside the hospital unsure, afraid. We had been through this before.

The heart monitor was beeping, 84, 88, 96, 120, 78. She was so tiny on the hospital bed, wearing an oxygen mask and oxygen tubes. Family, grandchildren, Loved Ones, chummies sitting vigil, sharing stories and prayers. Time disappeared, days and nights blended together, not sleeping not awake—listening carefully to grandmother voices and stories only heard in the quiet hours between Elders. Nsyílxcn, Nłeʔkepmxcín, and english intertwined, and I could not decide when one language ended and the next began. Grandmother voices soothing, singing, praying. They talked softly, laughed loudly, and shared stories of long ago, long into the quiet hours of night.

"Jake!" Her voice was a raspy whisper.

"Mom, who's Jake?" I asked.

"He fell off his horse."

"He what?"

"Jake fell off his horse."

"Oh." I paused, then asked, "Is he gonna be okay?"

She shifted in her bed and her eyes opened. "You like cowboys! I know you do," she said. There was uncomfortable laughter in the room. She smiled then and blinked her fuzziness away. I could see she was suddenly awake.

"Oh, you!" I smiled back, happy because she was with us again. The next day she ate lunch and told stories.

Work, school, finals weighed on my mind. My aunt, one of two Nłeʔkepmx nurses in our community, spoke to me in the hallway. "She's been here so many times over the years. There is a really good chance that she will recover. It's been over twenty years. She's worried about all of you. If you can, tell everyone to leave the room so that you can have a few minutes alone. Talk with her and pray with her. If it really is her time, she needs to know you will be okay."

We'd been here in this hospital before, frightened. How could I know the burden my godmom carried? Her fear of leaving? She would continue fighting and her heart, mind, spirit, and body would remain in agony. I knew she would find wholeness again, in spirit.

"Mom…" I felt inadequate; my words always came out wrong.

She lay quiet, watching me. She was so tired. I reached for her hands, cupped their tiny, wrinkled dryness in my own. I had no words. I told myself, try. You have to tell her.

"Mom." I paused again, speaking slow and clear. "I love you with all of my heart."

"I love you too, Babygirl." I tucked the warmed, blue cotton hospital blanket around her body.

"Mom, I don't want you to worry about me. If you are ready to leave, I'll be okay. I promise. I will be okay."

"Babygirl, I'm going to get better, you'll see. We'll go to the rodeos this summer. We'll find you a cowboy."

"Mom, I don't need a cowboy."

"Babygirl, I don't want you to be alone."

"Mom, you're not a spring chicken anymore."

"But I want to be a spring chicken."

"Yes, I know you do."

We prayed together until the rest of the family arrived and then they prayed too.

going home

they came for her on horseback
one cold December morning.

they rode in the old way
travelling the back roads
across fields and along the lake.
it was a beautiful day.

fresh snow was falling,
huge flakes that blurred the vision
reflecting pure white light in millions of directions.
the land and rolling hills were clean with its radiance.

she was busy fixing her bed,
drinking her coffee
arranging the odds and ends
that cluttered her bedside table
as though they mattered.

her waist-length hair
braided into a single braid
sat neatly on one shoulder.

the pale green hospital gown she wore
hung long and billowy around her.
she'd returned to her child self.
her body tiny, bent over, weak.

she knew they were coming.
when the doctor came in
he checked her heart and asked,
"how're you feeling this morning?"

there was a warm comfortable energy between them
that only years of knowing one another could create.

"oh, i'm good. i'm going home today."
surprised, he looked at her,
not saying anything.

later, after she settled back into bed
and the doctor and nurses left the room,
she looked out the open window
into the brilliance of the day.

that was when they came for her
and this time she was ready.

come inside

i want to sit by your grave and weep,
feel the dust between my fingers,
feel the earth beneath my feet,
hear your voice on the breeze.

sit outside your house
with the horses.

i want to sit at your grave and cry,
lay on tmíxʷ by your side,
cover myself in a blanket of dust,
hear the creak of the gate,
the whistle of the magpies flying by.

i want to pull up outside your house,
hear the dogs barking, the TV blaring
knock on your door
and know that you're going to be the one
opening it with your eyes surprised.

"Babygirl, come inside."

sit next to you on your old couch,
hold your hands in mine,
smell the awful stench of your cigarettes.
cook fish and rice,
sit down at the kitchen table and eat with you.

i want to throw myself on the kitchen floor,
demand, cry, holler.

"Mommy,
take me with you."

but you left us for good, this time.

wildflowers

through fields of wildflowers all in bloom
a kaleidoscope of blues
i watch your spirit leave
with the sunrise

it lights up the sky,
a flaming light
across our valley.

a million sparkles across our lake
i'm not sleeping i am awake.
waiting for the daybreak star
to show her beautiful face.

i want to tear down these walls,
set this world aflame
dust and ash falling
clogging the air that i breathe.

i want to smash every cup,
every bowl, every plate,
until the broken shards of memories
are on the floor around me.

rain falling, tmíxʷ beneath my feet
as the sun rises the roots continue to grow
binding to my feet
wild rose, juniper, cedar, and fir boughs
merímstn re-awakening

nkéxʷ

we walk to the creek behind the house
not far from where it joins the river.
the fresh chill of a winter bath beckons as we go.
the dogs, two brothers follow in rough tumbling play.

heart thick like nkéxʷ   a type of pudding
stewed scáqʷm & ɬk̓ʷəpn   saskatoon berries and bitterroot
bitterroot and berries,
flesh scraped raw like hide.
this throat is full of ash and stone.

if my body is a sweatlodge,
the seasons have worn it down
each red willow rib broken,
cover blankets rotten
fallen to the ground,
overgrown with spiders, ants, mice.

i wait for spring thaw flood waters
to wash it away,
thick and dirty as it goes.

if i could speak your names i would, but you rest.
if the land could answer my questions, I would ask
for all the medicines forgotten, songs misplaced,
for our languages and sacred teachings to return
to our lips, to our hands, to our hearts, to our minds.

i am
thankful for your songs,
for your stories,
for your teachings.

i am
broken, so broken
when, one by one, you leave.
we sing our sorrow as
the ancestors sing their joy.

tmíx^w

dedicated to Elders Mary & Ed Louie

after you left
the ancestors gathered

shadows woven into trees
along the fields,
beside the creek.

overcome
by the weight of
shattered stone,
heart spirit mind.

i snuck into the berry patch,
fingers and mouth greedy
for the roundness of berries.
the ancestors met me there.

the ancestors followed me
everywhere.

qʷənqʷént and heartbroken   pitiful
all i could do was yémit.   pray
leave the berries fat and hanging,
mouth dry from wishing.

it is good to suffer, sometimes.

on our knees,
forehead immersed within
a blanket of fir boughs,
sweltering.

from tmíxʷ we came,
to tmíxʷ we return,
Grandfather stones hot red
within woman medicine lodge.

four rounds of yémit & merímstn   prayers and medicine
sage, fir, wild roses, cedar, buckbrush,
praying, singing until the blanket lifts
and between each round:

"you girls g'wan, do your dunks.
surrender it, surrender all of it
sadness sickness sorrow
wash it away."

on tiptoe we cross ice and snow
water earth and sky pay witness

this body is a mountain
this body is the land

an echo of our Grandmothers,
feet immersed, rooted within
pebbles and sand.

péye?, séye?, ke?łés, mús.   one, two, three, four
creator ancestors witness.
this healing. this lifting,
this transformation.

awakened. activated.

complete.

A Gathering of Stones

I was praying in my sleep. In my dream, I was asking the Creator for help when the sensation of small paws entering my bedroom and running across my carpeted floor woke me. Then something landed on my chest. I couldn't see it but the paws running up, down, and across my body told me that it was a cat.

The fourth time it ran across me, it turned and came towards me. I was warm and cozy with my blankets up to my chin and one hand on top. The sound of the cat faded in and out, staticky like an old-time television set with bad reception. It was a scene out of *The Twilight Zone*. Suddenly the reception became clear, and a grey cat magically appeared in front of my face, hissing. It bit my hand. Suddenly awake, I hollered, "Get out of here!" I flicked on my bedside lamp to look for it, but the image of it had disappeared. If that was a dream, it sure felt real. The time was 6:43 AM.

I left the light on and lay down again, the hairs on the back of my neck raised and my body tense. She'd owned a cat, Esther... Esther Johnson, the little old lady who had lived here before me. Esther's passing had made this subsidized apartment in East Van available. I knew her name because her mail was still coming: government mail, junk mail, lottery sweepstakes, and the weekly TV Guide. John, the building manager, said that a major stroke had partially paralyzed her. The apartment had been badly damaged by her wheelchair and had required major repairs. I was able to move in by January 1st. Esther had lived alone. She couldn't talk.

The building manager hadn't mentioned a cat, yet the cat hairs embedded in all the curtains told me she'd had one. The worn little scratching post outside my bedroom window told me she'd had one.

A loud noise shocked me awake the next morning. It was my apartment buzzer. When I answered, I heard a man's voice on the intercom.

"Come through the little gate," I said, still wearing my flannel red PJs. When he knocked, I held the door not quite open, not quite awake. Friendly, confident, and dark-skinned, he was wearing a uniform and carrying a beige medical case.

"Oh, I'm just here to check Esther's blood," he said, and pushed the door open as though familiar with the place. I stepped back.

"Esther? You're here to check Esther's blood?" Looking down, my hand reached for the back of my head.

"Yeah, are you her granddaughter?"

"No, I'm the new tenant." I could not believe this was happening. He gave me a questioning look. "Esther's gone."

"Oh? Will she be back soon?"

"Uh, she, um, she passed away."

He had a shocked look on his face. "She what?"

"She passed away. I'm the new tenant. I just moved in."

"When?"

"In December, sometime before Christmas." I did not say: within a week of my godmom.

"No one even contacted us."

"I'm sorry. Her mail is still coming here, too."

When he left I returned to my bed, eyes puffy, chest aching. I didn't want to wake up.

Walking from Commercial Drive to my apartment, I think about those two old ladies. I knew my godmom well enough to know that even from the spirit world, she would check on me. My tiny little godmom, she had probably befriended Esther in the spiritual realm. She probably even visited the local Value Village down the street. East Van is a place of restlessness. There must be plenty of spirits around, and she was probably talking with all of them. Giving them the what-for the way old ladies do. She hated seeing people suffer and would forget her own pain in order to make others laugh.

My truth: No one will ever call me Babygirl ever again. No one will ever light up for me the way my godmom did. My truth: I am filled with shame for being selfish, for leaving the hospital. I should have been stronger. My truth: I am alone and I feel so lost. My truth: I want to give up. I've relapsed into suicidal ideation. Contemplation. Planning suicide feels like an addiction. It feels melodramatic. I just want to stop hurting. Is it possible to overcome? At some point I have to make a decision to heal. Enough is enough.

When I see them, they are perfect. Sunlight bursts through the branches and leaves, iridescent on the pink cherry blossoms. The path is illuminated in pink. Every year, springtime and cherry blossoms always remind me of UBC. There was a bunch of us students working in the First Nations Longhouse student lounge and one of our guy friends told all of us to stand beneath a huge cherry blossom tree across the street. All of us from the student lounge exited the building, walked across the grass, and stood beneath the tree. He climbed up high inside the tree and shook the hell out of it. Pink blossoms fell all around us and we danced among them. Laughing as blossoms fell in our hair, on our lips, and at our feet.

Indigenous students representing Nations all across British Columbia and Canada are here at UBC. We are all in different stages of our studies: forestry, education, fine arts, natural resource management, science, medicine, archaeology, anthropology. Not one of my new friends went untouched by sorrow during our studies. When you're Native, sometimes death comes in waves. It hurts to breathe. It hurts to think. It hurts to exist. Sometimes it's hard to imagine a time without grief. When you're Native, sometimes it feels like everywhere you turn, there are Loved Ones in mourning. At some point in our post-secondary studies, every single one of us students returned to our home communities to honour Loved Ones who had left this world. Some were due to natural causes or health issues; others were because of vehicle accidents. Too many of us lost Loved Ones to suicide, violence, or addiction. Each of us returned to UBC broken inside, but we persevered. We continued moving forward, doing the best we could. Sometimes loss is really hard and becomes all-encompassing. And we have to take time to recollect ourselves, to remind ourselves of where our blood comes from. To reconnect to our homelands, find safety and solace in the arms of our Grandmothers and Grandfathers in order to heal, and then eventually to return.

My godmom. My little brother. My grandpa. My dad. The Creator took each of them at different stages of their lives. Their names remain even though their spirits are gone. Each time, a blanket of sorrow covered our family. And each time, the healing process was different. Healing from grief does not happen overnight. Sometimes, honouring every single teardrop can feel like honouring a four-year-long thunderstorm of torrential rain. Healing is possible; it just takes time. Sometimes that means abiding by our healing ceremonies and our traditional grieving practices, but also honouring who we are today, as human beings in a contemporary world. And just because someone says it is traditional to not show emotions that does not mean we have to stifle our grieving. Honouring our Loved Ones who have left this world means we honour our grief no matter what shape it takes, as long as we are safe. And then, when it's time, we must learn to put the blankets of grief away.

Suicide. Where did I learn to think like this? I remember my godmom in the hospital bed when I was a child. She had taken too many pills. It wasn't the only time. She gave her love openly to all children; she adopted nieces, daughters, nephews, sons. Her love was limitless like the sky, like the land. She always did her best to lift others up. To help anyone who was hurting or suffering. Above all, she wanted all her children to live in a good way. She loved the children she lost in the fire. Did she learn to love herself? Why did she consider suicide an option? Where did she learn that? Did she suffer so deeply because of Indian Residential School? Her own grief and trauma? I am so relieved for her grandchildren that she recovered from that stage of her hurt, and that we were able to share a lifetime with her. I am so grateful that my godmom was so generous with her love, and that she chose to share her love with me.

The body is organic. It returns to tmíxʷ but where does the spirit go? In my imagination, I visualize the spirit as a perfect orb of light inside a flesh human body. Her spirit was pure, absolute perfection, like my brother and grandfather. The child inside me still wants to need her, but I know she is at peace with her Loved Ones and our ancestors. Healing means letting go of old coping mechanisms that just didn't work and learning how to live in a healthy way. Healing means overcoming hurt, abandonment, and behaviours that were often learned as far back as Indian Residential School, and even prior to that, when the diseases brought by contact arrived in our lands and decimated our people. Healing and transformation means relearning healthy ways to live and grieve; healthy ways to love and carry on. It means having endurance to carry on towards our personal vision of transformation when we reach the most difficult points in our lives. This is our journey today. To live and be free.

—

The cat was sitting on my chest, hissing. I opened my eyes, afraid. It scratched at my hand, and there was a momentary flash of pain. Somewhere inside me, I realized that the cat was suffering too. I knew it couldn't hurt me. It hissed. It was fluffy and grey. Maybe it's hungry. I could give it a bowl of milk and some salmon. But if I fed it, it might keep coming back. The last thing I needed was a pet ghost cat meowing me awake in the middle of the night, waking me up because it was hungry. It was just looking for Esther.

"Kitty, Esther's not here."

"Hiss. Sssssss."

"Kitty, kitty—aw, geez, kitty. Esther's not here, I'm sorry. I can't help you. You gotta go look for her in the spirit world."

It started meowing then, sad meows, lost kitty meows, and in a state of not sleeping and not awake, halfway between here and somewhere, I realized that I had better have a chit-chat with Esther too.

"Esther, you better come and get your cat." Then I fell back asleep.

A few days later, I had an opportunity to visit with a Skwxwú7mesh Elder. He came and prayed in my home. We had a conversation about the spirit world and the journey our ancestors make when they cross over to the other side. I honestly think he thought I was crazy, dreaming about a dead cat. But after he left, I burned sage and prayed: prayed for the kitty, prayed for Esther, prayed for my godmom. I prayed for their journey to the spirit world, that my joy for her would set her free, and that my grief would not keep her here. I also picked up a new book written by a Tibetan monk named Sogyal Rinpoche. It is a book about living and dying. The title sounded beautiful, like it would have stories that I needed to hear.

When I contemplate my understanding of the Nsyílxcn word, merímstn, I think of things that provide healing such as the medicine harvested from plants, trees, bushes for the kwílstn, the sweatlodge. It brings up treasured memories of my beautiful Elder and the crystal-clear creek flowing by her lodge. This is the same merímstn we use to wash our homes. I think of merímstn as medicine, as the elements that heal us. I am not a fluent speaker of Nsyílxcn; I have broken interpretations and limited understanding. I piece Nsyílxcn and Nłeʔkepmxcín words together like a jigsaw that quite possibly aggravates my Elders. So I also think of true love as merímstn, the compassionate, unconditional love of Elders, the love of children, and when parents know how to love. The merímstn brought by the Skwxwú7mesh Elder who visited my home were his healing words and teachings, his kind loving heart, and his presence. He reminded me how to be strong. He reminded me that I'm not alone. He reminded me that I am strong.

Merímstn: Cedar, wild rose bush, juniper, and fir boughs roll to a boil in a tall black pot on my stove. The steam awakens mountain ancients, and they break trail through my home. I stand over the pot, and the fragrant steam of the merímstn cleanses not just my face and neck but also my heart, mind, and spirit. Back home, my aunties, our aunties, everyone's aunties always help clean the house, wash everything with medicine water, usually four days after someone has crossed over to the spirit world. It washes away the essence of their energy and it clears the path for their journey to the spirit world. I was told that it's important not to hold on to too many things. In order for joy to return, you have to put away the sorrow. When you're ready, put it inside a cedar box and put the box away. Wrap it up inside a sacred bundle, bring the bundle to the mountain. Some sacred bundles you keep forever; some need to be put away.

I fill my green bucket two-thirds full of hot tap water, then add medicine water. I begin by washing the living room floors, then start on the walls, one room at a time until the whole place is clear. A dear Elder said, "If it's been sitting unused for a year or two, then you should let it go." Memorabilia that no longer serves a purpose, old clothes that I never wear, gifts that I never use. Garbage bag in hand, I walk from one room to the next, gathering the things that I need to let go of. The first item to go into the dumpster is kitty's scratching post.

When my grandpa left, the grief was heavy and the world went dark. I didn't want to live, not another moment, not another day.

After some time passed, I volunteered to be a driver for two of my Elders whom I had sat beside in the winter dance on many winter nights—so that they could attend the BC Elders Gathering in Prince George. They talked about so many random things. They were silly, they were spiritual, and when they didn't want me to know, they would speak in our language. When we returned home, my Elder told me to pull over beside Nicola Lake. And when we were there, he told me, "Go pick up some stones and make yourself a circle over there," he gestured to the water, "and you sit there." After a few minutes passed, he came over. "You think about all those things you're carrying. It's time to put them away now. Throw those stones back in that water now. You let it go now."

How could I have forgotten that there was another time. After my brother left, that summer, a dear Loved One brought me to sit with her at the creek beside her sweatlodge. "I want you to go pick out some stones there by my creek. It doesn't matter how many you gather. For everything that burdens your heart, mind, and spirit. For your sister, for your brother, for your mother, your godmother. I don't care if you have one hundred stones sitting there. Choose a stone for every piece of sadness, for the worry you have for your sister, for your broken heart. Give every stone a name. Tell me when you're done." When I was finished, she sat with me, there on the ground. Asked me to tell her who and what each stone represented. With each story, she held it in her hands, talked to every single stone, and then she created a circle with those stones. When we were finished, she told me, "Now we're going to put it all away. You have to throw each one into the creek. And as you pick up each one, you think about what you told me. What it represents. Let this be your prayer for healing. It is time to let it all go now."

My home is a gathering place for stones. Stones line all my windowsills, sit alongside my bathtub, gather on my bedside table. Stones that I've found along trails, beside rivers. I carry my favourite stones in my purse or the back pocket of my jeans. They are of all colours and shapes. Some are clear, some have rings, some are crystals, some are translucent. Stalactite, stalagmite, pipestone, soapstone, black obsidian. Rose quartz, citrine, tiger's eye, jasper, amethyst, moonstone, bloodstone, Fraser River jade. Touching the soft, smooth surface gives me enough merímstn to get through each day. Some represent memories I hold on to and the shadows of grief and despair that I can never let go. The part of me that I keep buried; doors inside my mind that I will never open again. The places where I store my grief, shame, abandonment, and loneliness. Walking from room to room, I reflect on every stone. So many years of collecting stones, representing every single season. How could I forget about their stone ceremony? My Elder, gone now. At the time he shared his teachings, I didn't quite understand his intention, but when the weight lifted, the relief was tangible. Beloved Nłeʔkepmx mentor—how could I forget the words she had shared with me so long ago?

the riverbed is home

she collects stones everywhere she goes.
stones in her pockets, stones in her coat,
stones in her purse, stones in her shoes.
they curl up like kittens in her sleeves
and rest in the back pockets of her jeans.

stones from the highest alpine, stones from the river bottom.
they bathe in the light of the sun
and wash in the rains when they come

Scẃéxmxuym̓xʷ, Spaxomin, Similkameen, Syílx temxulaxʷ
Secwepmx tmíxʷ Sptétkʷ, Coquihalla, péłuskʷu,
Stó:lō temexw, Chiyo:m, Sqew'qeyl,
Sk̲wx̲wú7mesh temíxw,
Batoche, Saskatoon, Prince Albert,
Saskatchewan.

she talks to stones because
they are closer to her than anyone.
she caresses them, breathes into them.

granite, jade, rose quartz, stalactite, obsidian,
soapstone, sandstone, pipestone,
spotted rocks, rocks with holes, rocks with rings.

her home is a riverbed, stones in her bath,
stones in her bed, stones along windowsills.
a blanket of stones to keep warm.

surrounded with a circle of stones
stones representing sorrow, representing grief
stones representing joy, laughter, deceit,
stones representing mothers, fathers,
stones representing sisters, brothers.

but the burden of carrying stones grows
with each passing day.

ancient mountain songs they sing
until she fills her pockets full of stones.
like berries they rest in her cedar basket
until her basket overflows.

she tosses her stones back in the river
because it's time to let them go.
Grandmothers praying,
Grandfathers singing

the river welcomes her children home.

this body
is a mountain,
this body is the land

as sisters

we walk along this Stó:lō riverbed,
the air fresh with rainfall and warm sunshine.
springtime has passed and summer draws to a close.

raindrops converge into streams, weaving across the flats
gathering in turquoise pools
small and big around the stones.

we are free to bathe here
lay among the ancients,
river rocks heated by the summer sun.
watch clouds move across the sky

we search for silence
in a place of echoes

young voices rising singsong
the noise of vehicles roaring past
a hawk's whistle as it dives

pay witness as red ochre
nestles amongst
stones, pebbles, sand, water.

our troubles are raindrops
gathered in pools. Full,
with story, song, and medicine.

we break trail everywhere we go
except here on this riverbed where
the rage of spring thaw high waters,
having retreated,
cut this wide path that we now follow.

Scẃéxmx

the People of the Creeks
this valley is our home.

tiny flames dance upon our skin,
dust devils gather within the sage.

highway 8 follows the curves of the land,
terraces of clay, sand, and stone.
if we could hear the words spoken by the land,
what stories would the land orate?

this valley is a pathway our river a channel from one nation to the next.
Thompson River green joins the Fraser, brown.
the Nicola and Coldwater rivers are our tributaries.

—

yémit   pray
yémxne   someone is praying for someone or something

yémxne e tmíxʷ   pray for the land
yémxne e qʷuʔ   pray for the water
yémxne
for the four-legged,
the winged, the ones that crawl and swim.

we yémit as we gather,
harvesting
the riches of our land, tmíxʷ.

we are
blessed by the air,
cleansed by the water,
nourished by the land.

we are
prepared to face a brand-new day.

May 20, 2000
Journal Entry

They are seated in a big semicircle around the room, speakers and microphones in key places throughout. Whether it is the Assembly of First Nations or BC Chiefs' Summit. Hereditary leadership, matriarchs, women and men, chiefs, councillors, youth and Elders, Indigenous leaders travel here from all across British Columbia and Canada. Some come to criticize. Some come to complain. Some come to gather, visualize, and strategize new beginnings. I love coming to these meetings and sitting on the bleachers. Along with other youth sitting around the room, together we pay witness.

Every time I hear they are gathering at the Chief Joe Mathias Centre, I come down. Why? The power of their visions, their determination, listening to our chiefs negotiating, troubleshooting, arguing, and strategizing. Listening to the deep love for our children, our Indigenous communities, and our future generations. The energy, even when it is fragmented, is so strong and so deep. I realize that every single one of us in the room, young and old, has committed our lives to creating positive change and healing within our communities in different ways. It's true, the chiefs don't always get along, and that's really annoying. But what matters is that every time the chiefs gather, it is with prayers in their hearts.

Listening to the words shared across the floor reminds me why I came to university. It puts me back on track when I am feeling discouraged, lost. It reminds me why I stay, despite the loneliness and detachment of campus and city life. It reminds me that the work I am doing is important not just for me, but for our future generations.

Reflecting on the work of our leaders at these meetings gives me courage to persevere even during the hardest moments of grief. The days when all I want to do is give up, not just on my studies, but on life. Witnessing our leaders and Elders at work helps me focus on what is most important, and that is not me. It's our youth and Loved Ones. It is that little ounce of strength that my work might one day offer to other young people. It makes me reflect on our Elders and ancestors, how they gave everything they had to bring our teachings forward for future generations.

For this reason, I know that no matter how hard the struggle, we can never give up. Our ancestors survived much harder times than these.

Adanac Trail

The gate swings shut as I walk down East Georgia Street past my cool white Pontiac Sunfire. My world has changed, and my godmother has left us to walk on our own. The annual orbit of the sun normally resulted in seasonal travels to harvest and preserve berries, fish, and deer; as well as travelling to ceremonies and to sober dances at the North Shore Alano Club; and visiting Loved Ones throughout Nłeʔkepmx territory, Secwepmx territory, occasionally over to Sx̌ʼax̌ʼimx and Lílwat and then Syílx temxulaxʷ, including the Similkameen, all the way back around to the territories of the Tsleil-Waututh, Skwxwú7mesh temíxw, Xʷməθkʷəyʼəm, and the city of Vancouver. However, my beloved car is dead in the street. I have been forced to still myself and sit in the centre of my grief. February has lost the battle and winter is ending. Creator kwulencuten's blessings of love and fury have broken up the ice and now the high mountain snow begins melting. Once again, the land is awakening to spring. A torrential, thunderous cleansing saturates absolutely everything. Tmíxʷ sings the most beautiful songs of the land and mountains breathing, reclining, arising, awakening to the changing of seasons.

Spring comes early on the West Coast, and when the world awakens, the only trail that matters to a paddler is the wake marking the passage of our canoes. It is time to train. All the paddlers on the land rise to the call. Minds, bodies, and spirits hunger for the stretch and pull of cedar blades reaching and gathering water; the rip and tear of muscles and tendons growing. I watch a female cyclist zip past as I continue to trudge along the street. That cyclist is stronger cycling up the hill than I feel going down. I own a bike, but I'm scared to ride it. If I rode my bike, I would save so much time. If I rode my bike, I would be strong. My steps are heavy and I feel weak as I run to catch the bus on Commercial Drive. Too soon, the bus arrives, and I'm still running. It glides through a puddle, narrowly missing me, and continues down the street without stopping. The sky is a ceiling of falling silver ribbons. I have been lax. I have been lazy, and I have become stale in the funk of my grief and depression. I know how it feels to be physically strong. I know what I need to do. The season is changing, and it is time for an awakening.

The first budding leaves unfold themselves into the glory of spring, and the grass is growing. The rain has created a sea of emerging greenery. When I was younger, my counsellor explained that being healthy meant balancing all elements of my life: mental, physical, emotional, and spiritual. This year, I have realized that as an intergenerational survivor of Indian Residential School, I am also surviving the genocide of my ancestors. I am not alone on this path, yo-yoing between suicidal thoughts, depression and my efforts to gain physical and intellectual strength. This healing journey is not an individual thing. It is the healing of all the generations that have gone before and all the generations that will come after. It is the healing of my children. Our ancestors broke this trail, and it is our job to maintain it. We carry a burden that is so much greater than ourselves. We continue the work of our ancestors, moving towards the healing and transformation of our lives for the benefit of future generations. So that, like our ancestors, our future generations can live blessed by heartfelt peace, joy, health, and abundance. The way they were meant to live.

"Draw the medicine wheel and map out all four realms: mental, spiritual, emotional, physical. Freewrite about how they are reflected within your life." It's true; the teachings of the medicine wheel are not Salish. I am not certain, but I suspect that the teachings embedded within represent a compendium of other teachings from a multitude of Indigenous Nations. It has worked for people like me who needed a methodology, a map to follow to gain courage and skills to recover from the hurt of the past. Along with the guidance of my Elders, it has helped me transform my life. This journey of healing and transformation is different for everyone.

It is a lifelong process of steadfast learning, strategizing, and actively employing new skills. Staying consistent, being self-observant and self-aware of internal struggle, because quitting and self-sabotage can no longer be part of the equation. Shame-based thoughts, like tape recordings on repeat, falsely told me, "You're nothing but a loser, a failure. You're not worthy of love." But none of that is true. I am worthy. I am not a failure. I am capable. I am intelligent. I know what it takes to be strong. And I can achieve this goal of graduating from university.

I chose to quit drinking in my teens because I came to believe that everything painful that I had witnessed or experienced as a child had been linked to someone's addictions. Leaving that stage of life behind was my first step toward creating, and learning to live, a happier, healthier life. Now I also understand that all the issues interwoven with alcoholism and addictions are deeply interlinked with intergenerational grief and trauma resulting from colonization.

Genocide. The Truth and Reconciliation Commission of Canada called it "cultural" genocide, but the genocide was not limited to an attack on Indigenous culture. It was a strategic attack on an entire group of people. The original people of this land now called Canada. So many strategic actions and so many layers of loss. The theft of women and children, the theft of land, the theft and destruction of resources, including the destruction of entire water bodies and ecosystems critical to Indigenous subsistence economy. Indian Reservations, created with laws enforced that denied "status" Indigenous people the right to leave the reserve and travel throughout their traditional territories in order to hunt, trap, fish, and harvest food. Our grandmothers and grandfathers could no longer access and cultivate the bountiful abundance of riches from the sacred tmíxʷ temexw temxulaxʷ that had always nourished and sustained our ancestors. Despite our inherent responsibility to take care of the land and all of its resources, every element of Indigenous seasonal rounds related to the harvest and provision of traditional foods and medicinal plants was controlled and forbidden. This resulted in severe poverty, disease, malnutrition, and starvation.

Entire communities of Indigenous children stolen at gunpoint and forced into Indian Residential Schools, into foster homes, exposed to disease and sexual and physical violence. Children deprived of safety, deprived of love, deprived of food. A graveyard outside of every single Indian Residential School in Canada means well over 139 graveyards for Indigenous children.

In Stó:lō temexw—the Fraser Valley, British Columbia—this included the theft of children by miners during the gold rush. The rampant theft of children from the time of contact left entire communities across the country barren of laughter, barren of love. The theft of children resulted in two generations of my family being taken away. Babies and children need love to survive and so do adults. Canadian government policies stated that their intention was to "kill the Indian and save the man." "Save the child" by denying Indigenous children the physical, emotional, and spiritual safety of a loving family. "Save the child" by starving children in nutrition experiments conducted without their parents' consent. And then silently and secretly burying children without ever telling their families. Canada. Can you imagine a country without children? A country barren of the sound of children's voices crying, laughing, making sing-song as they called out for their yéye?s and spápze?s As they cried out the names of their brothers, sisters, and cousins? The only thing left within our Indigenous communities was the echoes of silence. These are the blankets of sorrow; these are the layers of grief and loss that today's generations are working so desperately to lift. This is our journey as Indigenous people. Recovering ourselves, our families, our communities, our cultures, recovering our secret and sacred places, recovering our songs and traditional names. Recovering the ability to live, love, and experience joy without shame.

"During the time of deepest grief, don't let your mind get away with you, especially at night. Don't believe the nighttime thoughts." These words, spoken during a time of great sorrow, were shocking at first and required self-reflection. In that process, I realized that it was during the late-night hours of insomnia when I struggled the most with depression, hurt, worthlessness, and self-hatred. It was during those hours that I contemplated and planned my suicide. It was during the late-night hours of grief and aloneness when my heart and spirit felt most vulnerable.

How does a person recover from grief? How do you overcome a lifetime of depression and begin healing?

The answers shared by many included: Find a good counsellor or therapist and make sure any therapist you see is actively engaged in their own personal healing. Research the places that offer support: on campus, at the community health centre, friendship centre, or at a counselling referral agency. Organizations that focus their programming on survivors of Indian Residential Schools have a better understanding of the needs of Indigenous clients healing from intergenerational trauma. Consistently and regularly attend appointments with therapists. And be alert to the red flags. If at any point you feel unsafe or judged by the counsellor, find someone else.

Emotional and spiritual healing is not an overnight process. It takes self-discipline, endurance, and courage to rise. Seek out sacred and safe spaces: land, mountains, water, people. Cedar, fir, or juniper trees will always welcome you within their boughs and cover you with their unconditional love. Paddle to a secluded beach, run or walk a mountain trail, walk them all. Endorphins are an essential element of joy. Go to the water to pray and brush off the negative energy, listen and sing the songs of our homelands. Rain or shine, get out on the land. If not, go to the gym. Shake it off, sweat it off. Crack your own whip and bust your own ass, especially when you're sinking. Find ways to create the healing energy you need to keep going. Spend time on the land harvesting traditional foods. Find a safe place by clear, moving water, and do those four dunks that our Elders have taught us to do. The task is to create a wellness plan and follow it. To meditate and pray with every step that touches the ground, with every reach and pull of the paddle. The task is to do what it takes to stay alive and to transform the hurts of the past into a source of strength.

Go to the homes of beloved Elders and clean their kitchens. Every stage of cleaning helps clear the mind of negative energy. Our Elders taught us to work hard, keep our hands busy, keep our minds busy. And it's okay to have a bad day. Falling off the path doesn't mean it's the end; it just means you have to dust yourself off and start again. Every moment is a chance to remember, to reset, and to start again.

At canoe practice, Coach once said, you can't quit paddling when you're tired, especially if you're in the middle of the lake or on the ocean. If you run as far as you can in one direction, you still have to turn and run, walk, or paddle home. Everything in life is about self-discipline, and our ancestors lived by these laws to survive. Those original teachings of self-discipline, as taught by our Elders and sacred Knowledge Carriers, are what we must return to in order to recover ourselves.

In the city, it can be hard to maintain balance. Trudging a street surrounded by cement and manicured lawns forces a person to get creative to stay fit. Growing stale due to inactivity is not an option. I fish my cellphone out of my coat pocket, pick away the lint, and scroll through my contacts list until my mechanic's phone number pops up. "Hi, Ron. You mentioned you had a buyer for my Sunfire? Yes, please, I want to get rid of it. Sure, I'll take that. Do you have a tow truck? Awesome." A few hundred will cover rent, food, and bills. That's my priority. That lime-green and blue road bike has been gathering dust in the junk room for too long. It's not going to dig itself out. Shred anxiety and just ride. YES, the car is dead. Road trips are not an option. Driving to the grocery store or to North Van for a ride on my canoe in Tseil-Waututh is not an option. Beached. Ride, walk, or catch a bus across the Second Narrows

Bridge to visit my canoe—it's too far to run. Transformation requires endurance and steadfast motivation.

Amidst cigarette butts and banana peels left by my upstairs neighbours, I lace my shoes, then stretch calves, back, quads, hammies, and do a few squats and lunges. I try to look like I know what I'm doing. A cumbersome, tin can tread leads past telephone poles and bushes and beneath blossoming cherry trees. Strategy: Run and walk from one telephone pole to the next. East Georgia over to Venables; walk and run the hill all the way to Trout Lake. This is the shedding of skins: the death of the grieving body and rebirth of a living body. A loving heart is the feeling that comes as sorrow releases its hold. My canoe is calling. The tug, push, and pull of cedar all around me, digging my blade into the waves: complete transformation. I need to feel a different kind of pain, the kind from muscles stretching, flexing, and growing. This is the kind of pain that will make me strong again.

East Van is stink, with the chicken factory down the road and the occasional rotten chicken part lying on the street in front of the factory. When the breeze is "right," it smells like stink chicken any day of the week. I never thought I'd attend university and live in East Vancouver, down the road from a chicken factory. Persevere. My ancestors survived much harder times than this. I can and I will complete this degree.

When I dig out my road bike, both tires are flat. But that's not the end. I wipe off the dust and walk it the few blocks to the bike store where they inspect my tires and lube the chain. When I pick it up, it rolls smoothly on the street. It doesn't make sense to walk my bike, so despite growing anxiety, I give it a try. The wheels are so narrow I can hardly balance on the seat. The gear tension isn't right, so my feet swing around the pedals way too fast. I adjust the gears and keep going. Riding it up a hill for the first time is ridiculous. The bike wobbles, and I have to pedal harder so I can stabilize with my legs and stomach muscles. Beyond terrified and self-conscious of all the passersby, I ride around the block until I can maintain my balance. These Italian road bike tires are super fast and today, I feel like a super geek.

Every day and every week, muscles continue to reawaken and grow with the awakening of spring. The running has helped, now the bike. A few blocks at a time with distance consistently lengthened. It's easy to get lazy and it's easy to quit, so every time I start feeling depressed and toxic thinking slips in, I put on my workout gear and go for a run or go for a ride. My goal is to ride across the Second Narrows Bridge all the way to Tsleil-Waututh. I run as far as possible in one direction, with the knowledge that at the end, I have to turn and run all the way home. Just like when I am paddling. I paddle to the end of the lake, or around the islands by Deep Cove, then turn and paddle all the way back to the beach. I buy a really good double bike lock from a bike store on Commercial Drive. Every day, I ride my bike a little bit farther until I decide to start riding to the university. I ride my bike to Commercial and East Broadway, then throw it on the bike rack for the trip up to campus, then cycle to class. Afterwards, I ride the city bike trails all the way home to Commercial and East Georgia.

She is there, the woman on the bike who blazed past me in the rain. She gave me the inspiration to gather my courage and start riding. That woman bikes past almost every single day, to and from wherever she goes. Dusk on a spring night on my way back from campus. She's trying to pass me again. Amidst other cyclists on Adanac Trail, the decision is made. Today is not the day. Today, I'm not going to let her pass me by. She picks up speed; I push my bike pedals harder. My antique Italian road bike is fast, faster than her fancy new one. She pushes even harder; I can hear her breathe. On the hillside going up, she goes for the pass. The muscles on her legs and forearms bunch as she stands and digs with her feet, pushing hard on her pedals. That's when I hit it even harder and give it everything I have. She paces me for the last five blocks, all the way up the hill to the street outside my building. When I pull over outside my place, she passes me and says, "Good race." I could cry because I am so proud of myself, but instead I just give her a nod and a wave.

—

The breeze picks up as I ride up East Georgia Street to Victoria and then from Adanac Trail to Sunset. My cedar canoe is stored beside the ocean in the community of the Tsleil-Waututh. I feel super fast on my road bike; strong, alive, and so electric. The bike trail leading up to the Second Narrows Bridge is steep. The rumble of a thousand vehicles is thunderous. Not the sound of torrential rain falling on the lake. Not the sound of a spring storm releasing. It is the artificial sound of machines, crashing and banging on the bridge as they cross the Indian Arm. The drivers of those vehicles do not care that this ocean, these waterways, this land is infused with the blood, the DNA, and the life force of a thousand generations of Indigenous people. As Indigenous people, we are fused with the life force of these waterways and this land. There is no ending, no beginning between us; we are the land, we are the water. We have journeyed this landscape, these water highways for millennia, and we will not stop. We can never stop. Wind from the ocean channel, wind from the mountains; the wind is the breath of our ancestors. The wind is endless like our blood, and like the wind, our spirits will carry on forever. This land and these mountains are woven with the bones and hair of our ancestors, and we will never leave.

Pushing, pulling, fighting, protecting, reclaiming. Transforming into power. Transforming into strength. We do not die. We cannot die. We cannot concede. We transform. Resurgence is our only choice.

Resurgence

The Trail

When I first moved to Stó:lō temexw, I dreamt I was travelling through the Coquihalla Mountains, with moccasins on my feet. The journey was long and the path wound through the mountains. A dry arid Southern Interior landscape of sagebrush, windswept yellow grass-covered hills, and willow bushes where coniferous lodgepole pine and subalpine fir became alpine meadows, gradually changing into ferns, brilliant green moss, and great, ancient cedar and douglas fir trees that grasped the sky. The breeze that whistled through the trees had a damp chill unlike the dry, dusty wind of home. A river flowed, a turquoise artery through tremendous walls of slate and stone that made the Coquihalla and Northern Cascade mountains. Far above—from the sky—I could see the trail extending into the distance.

Years later, while working in East Van there was a building I walked into—as part of the work, we did building and unit inspections. In the entranceway, my eyes beheld a black painting on a wall far above my head. The painting had one long red trail through the middle, extending from the bottom to the top like a road. There was an image of a person walking along that red road. All around in the blackness, images of humans stood, as though trapped, their bodies emaciated and suffering.

New in a way that I cannot explain, my eyes fresh as though having just emerged from the lodge, I looked up at that painting and remembered the dream. Seeing all those souls trapped in darkness brought a deep hurt to my heart, knowing that East

Hastings was only a block away. So many cousins, aunts, uncles, grandmas and grandpas, daughters and sons were there, trapped in a cycle of addiction and suffering. In my eyes, that is what the painting seemed to illustrate. How many of us had spent days and nights—even years—searching, crying, begging, and praying for the healing and recovery of our Loved Ones? The painting hurt because some of my dearest family members were perilously close to that. It made me pray harder for my family who struggled, as well as for all those I didn't know, those along Hastings Street. The painting seemed to represent everything those caught up in the most severe stages of addiction were facing.

Exiting the building, I tried to understand the artist's vision. Was it a warning? How did the residents of the building feel as they walked past it every day? Leaving it like that did not sit right with me. I wished I could take it down and with a fine-tipped brush, paint trails in red, gently showing them the way to the red road. Surround the trail with trees and mountains, bring in sunlight and a river so that those who were suffering could remember the gentle loving vibration of the land beneath their feet.

Stories Are Alive

When I was eighteen, I was still living with my sk̓ʷóz, my grand-auntie. Eighteen was the age I stopped drinking. The Nicola Valley Elders' Group was already diligently working towards revitalizing our Nłeʔkepmxcín language. I was able to travel with our Elders' group as a youth assistant to several language conferences. Eighteen and surrounded by a gang of Nłeʔkepmx yéyeʔs, I had many adventures with them, many moments with them laughing and talking vibrantly. I was a witness, and sometimes I comprehended their dialogue, observing as they shifted back and forth between languages: english, Nłeʔkepmxcín, some also speaking Nsyílxcn. Sometimes I asked for an interpretation, which I didn't always receive because…well, they would get crazy sometimes. Our first trip was to Hilo, Hawai'i. The world was humid in Hilo. Apparently, the Big Island has a dry side and a rainy side. It rained every night, and then come daylight the sun would shine brightly again. Our second trip was to Albuquerque, New Mexico. I shared a dorm room with my sk̓ʷóz in each destination and escorted her everywhere she went, or perhaps I should say, she escorted me.

The trip to Albuquerque was especially memorable because I had never really eaten Mexican food. The one staple food I recall on every table was beans. Back home, milk and anything dairy never went well for me. Winter, spring, or summer sk̓ʷóz would come into my room and tell me, "p̓w'əm, p̓w'əm! I can hear you! You'd better open your windows!" And then she would open them for me. Some days, I would exit my room into the living room, and she would have every single door and window open, even if it was the middle of winter with an ice-cold wind blowing through. "That fresh air is good for you, you know." Sharing a dorm room with my beloved skʷóz was an adventure. In Hawai'i, we had our Hawaiian chocolates, trinkets, and a miniature dancing hula girl. In New Mexico, we had beans. Ṗw'əm, ṗw'əm, ṗw'əm, we took turns tooting into the night. Unfortunately, in New Mexico she could not open the doors and windows.

A language conference near Seattle, Washington was our third trip together. An Elder—from the Lushootseed-speaking area near Seattle, I believe—was one of the keynote speakers. He stood out everywhere he went. His vibe, his physical energy, his hat and attire were distinct, and his body was lean. When he stood up to speak, I was captivated by the richness of embodied ancestral memory evoked through his oratory. I wished desperately for a pen and paper. I wished for the old-school photographic memory my Elders spoke so highly of, carried by those trained to remember. All while telling my mind: *Remember this! You can't forget this moment. You have to hold onto his words!* There were many things he spoke of. His knowledge of the land, his memories growing up as a fluent language speaker, and the reasons our traditional narrative practices and languages were critically important for the continuance of our traditional way of life and for future generations. He embodied the stories, his languages, teachings, and his homelands in a way that was tremendous and indescribable. I desperately held onto his words. In particular, he said

Our words are powerful! Our stories are elastic and our languages are music! The stories are alive and when they are released to the world, they come alive. They are a spirit within themselves, and we are only the channel that brings them to life. Like tiny beings, they dance, they move around and they enter us and that's when they do their work. They are medicine for our people. That's why, as artists, as story-tellers, we have to be careful about the stories we tell, and the words we speak because once we release them to the world, that is when they do their work.

Embodying the voices of the Old Ones, he fluently drifted between languages. Movements, expressions, profound intonations of voice made his time on the floor, orating, absolutely captivating, so much so, that I can still hear his voice in my mind. It has been over twenty-five years, and I continue to reflect on what he said, particularly when other Elders stand up and speak about responsibilities to the land, our languages, our stories, and our future generations.

Why Am I Writing This?

I'm writing to remember. I'm writing to reconnect the strands that should not have been broken. I'm writing to learn how to listen with my heart as well as to share our stories and our history in a good way, so we never forget who we are. This is one strand creating a narrative of strength, intertwining hearts, minds, and spirits, reminding ourselves of all that is good and strong. I'm writing to listen and remember the story echoes that are the voices of our ancestors as they sing back to us when we sing to the mountains, when we sing to the water, when we sing to the land. I'm writing to understand and reflect on Indigenous stories, so that our truths and our identity as Indigenous people can never again be wiped away by the colonizer.

As a young person, I didn't know how to cope with grief. In my lowest moments, most often at night, thoughts of self-degradation and toxic shame would take over. At some point while riding those waves, the questions and memories started coming. "When did I first learn about suicide?" "Is it me, or is it my mind that resorts to these thoughts?" "Why does healing take so damn long?" "I want to be better already. I want the pain to stop." "I want to make a change so that my siblings won't have to go through this."

"You have to retrain your brain." Those were my counsellor's words so long ago. Detach, ever so slightly from the mind, and reflect on how it functions. Sometimes it feels as though it is its own entity. That's when I realized it was like a child that didn't receive the consistent, unconditional love, validation, and support that it truly needed. That's when I realized I can give myself the consistent, unconditional love, validation, and support that I truly need. Through running, through paddling, through time on the land harvesting traditional plants and walking on mountain trails, I was able to find my feet and walk through my healing journey. The mind as well as the body, heart, and spirit need to be taught self-love. Safe love. Consistent love.

You are truly loved. You are worthy, and your healing journey is important for everyone around you. Your personal story of hurt and trauma is valid. Your healing, no matter how hard, no matter how messy and complex, will also be your transformation. For our children and future generations. For our Elders who are still suffering from unspoken hurt and trauma. Heal and learn self-love, for our parents and grandparents who never experienced true love, safe love, unconditional love, and most importantly, self-love.

Sometimes we spend days with Loved Ones, sometimes in ceremony. Sometimes at sunrise or sunset, yet, over and over again, we don't know they're suicidal until it's too late. Every year, there are brothers and sisters who give up on life instead of fighting for the strength and resilience to overcome despair. Is this possible? I truly believe it is. I believe we can make a decision to fight for our lives and for the lives of our Loved Ones. I believe we can heal, but we have to do the work to recover ourselves and our lives.

Our Indigenous family trees are absolutely enormous; combined, my maternal and paternal sides, as well as my stepdad's and my godmother's families number in the thousands. Grandpa had twelve siblings, and Grandpa had nine children, my mom being one of them. In a non-Indigenous family, there is significant separation, sometimes across continents, without contact. But when you are raised within an Indigenous community, family includes your longhouse family, adopted family. Indigenous third cousins become more like first cousins, and sometimes they are siblings. It includes the family of your cultural and ceremonial parents. When you are raised by your Elders, a community of Elders, when aunties, uncles, and grandparents are all involved in raising the children, cousins are siblings. And yes, when you are Indigenous, you can have multiple mothers and fathers, many who came to you through ceremony. So, when we talk about healing, every step has a resounding impact because we are so deeply interconnected. To our families, to our communities, to our Nations and traditional territories. To the teachings and cultural practices of our lands. When we choose to begin our healing journey, we create waves that inspire everyone around us. We don't realize how important this is until the children in our lives start following in our footsteps.

Run

To be an emotionally happy, healthy woman and mother in a colonial world, recovering from the intergenerational impact and inherited trauma from Indian Residential School: What does that look like? I am a mother, now in my mid-40s, working hard to take accountability for personal wellness in all realms as I understand them: physical, mental, emotional, and spiritual.

Strength in this generation means exercising indoors as well as outdoors. It means we choose to climb mountains not for survival, but for harvest and exercise, as well as transformative moments of reflection and connection. With the lockdowns and public health orders brought on by the COVID-19 pandemic, daily life changed significantly. I now participate in online CrossFit classes at home. Learning to weight train with the barbell and free weights, with coaches guiding the process, has been a lifelong dream. My goal is to learn to engage the movements properly and with confidence. Now, more than ever, wellness is fundamental, not just for my personal longevity but for the well-being of my children.

With this awareness comes my effort to teach my children how to take care of themselves. Cooking, cleaning up after themselves, taking care of our pets, and feeding themselves while balancing healthy and unhealthy food options. The addiction to digital devices and online gaming has been a struggle for us all, especially with school closures and community lockdowns. It's hard to feel like I'm doing this well. The hardest days are when I feel that I am failing. When I feel too stressed. When I have been alone as a mother for too many days, weeks, and months. Every room has a makeshift fort, dolls line the walls, socks are everywhere, the house is completely upside down, and I have chapters for my dissertation to submit. *Breathe! Just go for a run. We will get through this, one step at a time.*

I breastfed both my babies until they were over two, closer to three. My daughter, now six and in grade one, still sleeps with me. Parenting in a pandemic has been an ongoing navigation through waves of anxiety about providing for my children. There are messages I tell myself. Just do your best. Even when stressed, strive to do everything with love. Express your love for your children, not just with words but with actions. Remember to laugh and play with them. Remember to tickle them. Remember that food is medicine. Check their hair for nits. Check your own hair for nits, and panic for a few weeks if we all have nits. Clean the kitchen with love. Sweep the floors with love. Remember, you function happier as a mother when your home is tidy and your floors are, at the very least, swept. The condition of your home is a reflection of your heart and your mind. If you wash the dishes before bed, you know you will wake up to clean counters.

There are many nights when it has been all five of us sleeping in my room. My son on the single mattress beside my bed, my girl snuggled close, our golden retriever Sophie, and Mittens the kitten. Together we have a nice pajama party. We sleep better. I don't criticize myself for the moments that make my children feel safest and happiest. I reflect often on the words of one of my Elders. Her hands waving around, she spoke passionately, and her words help me feel at ease now.

A long time ago, we didn't leave our children alone at night. We kept them safe. We kept them warm. We never left the babies to cry by themselves. The grandmothers and aunties all helped. Residential schools changed all that; children were left alone to cry, and they weren't protected. Parents were shamed by the church for expressing love and protecting their children. Now you see all these people; they all still carry that hurt because they didn't receive love when they needed it most.

I don't send my son to sleep in his room. I haven't yet weaned myself from nights cuddling with my girl. As it was when they were nursing toddlers, here I am, the mother, who needs to be weaned from my children as they grow. Maybe it's guilt because I feel like I'm not enough. Like I haven't been able to give them enough. Me who needs to face the next stage of my Babygirl becoming a big girl. Our learning now shifts to one where I strive to understand and teach my children all about their power and gifts as human beings. How do I do this, without my beloved Elders who shaped me?

I Believe in the Power of Prayer

"You were sent away too many times. That's why it's difficult for you to return."

In the darkness on a winter evening, the words were spoken with sincerity. We sat talking about life things—for me, mother things, for her, grandmother things—while praying and searching for my sister. Our grandmothers were half-sisters, and she is an older generation than me. She carries one window to my history. Last summer, a childhood friend contacted me. "I was thinking about the times I spent with you when you were alone in Lower Nicola. It was so hard. I see you struggling right now. I hope it helps that I'm thinking about you. I do know parts of your history that help me understand. Back in the day, we didn't talk about the serious stuff. But it always was just an unsaid known, about how life was..." Aloneness. As a mother and a survivor, my mom worked hard to achieve all that she has. In the photos I see of her with me, she is so petite she looks like a child. Only a few short years after leaving Indian Residential School, she returned to school for her post-secondary degrees. I know that she felt tremendously alone and unsupported too.

At one stage, grief for my brother tore our family apart, and for each of us, it manifested differently. We each had all these waves—memories, grief, confusion, rage—to surf. There was a stage where many nights were spent in the rain outside Vancouver buildings. Sometimes I just prayed to get a glimpse of my cɔceʔ, who in that stage of her journey, had taken a life path that terrified us all. The hardest part was accepting how powerless we all were, when addiction ruled her life. I fantasized about doing an old-school heist. Enlisting the brute strength of cowboy cousins and uncles to come with their ropes and kidnap her, tie her up like a calf on branding day, and help me haul her home. I had a vision of bringing her up a mountain to some imaginary cabin. I'd build a sweatlodge by the creek and keep her there in ceremony, no matter how hard she fought, until she was clean and sober. I thought long and hard about the ways this could be turned into a script for a play, for no other reason than to illustrate my overwhelming feelings of powerlessness, wanting to embody a vision of healing and transformation. To fight the addiction, through mind, body, storytelling, and prayer.

Many days and nights passed when I was overcome by feelings of powerlessness and fear for her well-being. Prayer was all we had, and so that is what we did. We prayed for her, every single day. Just as my Elders taught me to do for my mom and my godmother as a child. With a smudge made of sage, cedar, and sweetgrass. In the sweatlodge. By the water. In the silence of our minds. Verbally with our Elders. I gave photographs of her to my Elders so they could pray too. When my sister returned, she made a commitment to her transformational journey. I am grateful for the courageous steps she has taken as well as the steadfast commitment she has for her healing journey. Her strength, her presence, and her healing journey is a blessing for all of us.

Prayer was all we had. I had a friend who raged at me for being a person who prays. He associated prayer with european religion, catholicism, and oppression. He said "that's not the bakwam way." Yet it is. Indigenous people have always been a prayerful people, but the places we went to pray, the ways we engaged in prayer and ceremony was not that of the church. Prayers represent love and gratitude as much as they are songs of celebration, feasting, and ceremony. My Elders taught me to have a prayerful mind as I cook. To be conscious of my thoughts and my words and my energy because our food represents our prayers. When we feed the people, our prayers for healing, joy, and well-being enter their bodies, hearts, minds, and spirits, and our beloved guests are nourished by them. Prayers represent the journey songs sung to bless a Loved One's journey to the spirit world or to places that require travel by car, plane, horse, or ocean canoe. Traditional dances also represent many things: acknowledging sacred trusts, governance and responsibility, or as healing prayers and deep physical connection to the heartbeat of tmíxʷ and all things belonging to tmíxʷ. Our existence and our cultural practices are one part of the sacred circle.

Every Indigenous Nation around the world has ceremony with distinct, diverse, and dynamic ways of interacting with spirit. I do feel nervous speaking about prayer because I carry my own memories, my own hurt, and at times, my own rage towards the colonial legacy of trauma and oppression that Indian Residential School left upon my Elders' and mothers' generations.

My Elders have always been prayer warriors. They pray in Nłeʔkepmxcín. They pray in Nsyílxcn. They pray in Halq'eméylem, Hə́ńq'əmińəm', Secwepemctsín, Sḵwx̱wú7mesh sníchim, Cree, Michif, and they pray in english. With eagle feathers and a smudge bowl of dried buffalo sage. They pray with candles and bowls of clear water. They pray with cedar, juniper, fir boughs, and pure intentions situated in love. They pray beside waterways and as we harvest plants and medicines. When I was young, I didn't understand why it was important to pray so often. Some of my earliest memories of my Elders praying are from under the kitchen table with my godmom nearby. I remember the prayer groups. The prayer circles and prayer meetings always started with visiting, and then the sermonizing would begin. A big thick copy of the old and new testament resting in my goddad's hand. My godmom also had her own. Filled with handwritten words on folded papers tucked inside the pages. I still have some of her notes just so I can touch the lines her hands drew.

We are now the second and third generations of those who survived Indian Residential Schools, and the trauma caused by child apprehension during the Sixties Scoop has continued into the present. As younger generations, we are unweaving colonial trauma, child apprehension and foster care, and religious memories while also witnessing our Elders as they untangle themselves. We have been child witnesses to our parents' journeys, many of whom are Elders or are at the doorway to Elderhood. Many of our Elders believed in jesus christ and that is how they found connection to their holy spirit. I am not a churchgoing person. I witness, honour, and support survivors for the positive ways they chose to fix themselves and survive the hardest years of their lives. So many of our people are carrying hurt. When our people pray, regardless of how they pray, I pray too, always, because I believe in the power of prayer.

> we are the ones.
> our children are the ones.
> our grandchildren are the ones
> our ancestors prayed for. persevered for.

We Are Their Prayers Come to Life

Steps landing on loose dust become a rhythm of heartbeats as we commence our climb on this grind of a mountain trail. Today, my dear friend and I are following a new path on a mountain we have never climbed before. One step after another, with breath heavy, we surge forward despite the quickly rising incline. With strong and able bodies, we move with the lay of the land. In some areas, dust rises in clouds with every step. In some areas, the soil is fine, like silt, and our feet slide downward, erasing any sign of our presence. In other areas, tmíxʷ is dark brown and compact, smooth from the many runners who ran this trail before us. We carry on within the shade of trees, acknowledging ferns, mushrooms, various blossoms, and ripened berries. It's a reciprocal exchange. The land gives off a charge of energy that tmíxʷ channels through our lungs. We breathe out; the trees breathe us in. As mothers, we strive to overcome the burdens within our hearts, minds, and history, surpassing barriers laid down long before our feet were set upon tmíxʷ.

Back and forth the grind weaves us upward through the trees. A rocky outcrop, loose gravel. Sharp-edged stones roll beneath our feet then tumble away because we are sure-footed today. When we reach the viewpoint, Stó:lō temexw extends out before us. It is a warm day and the sky is clear. Had Sema:th Lake not been drained, we'd have the perfect view of its wide expanse encompassing much of the valley floor. I imagine it reaching almost to the base of the far mountains, extending across the 49th parallel, into what is now Washington, USA. Stó:lō fishermen would be training their children to fish on shovelnose canoes, with nets and spears, all made from cedar and perhaps various types of hardwood and stone.

My maternal grandmothers are from a valley two hours east of our current location. A place of little rainfall, the world is a tinder landscape all year around. A feast of traditional foods mainly involves a variety of springtime shoots and roots or whatever happens to be in season—preserved tea and berries, the four-legged, the freshwater swimmers. My friend's Lummi ancestors are from a place southwest of here. Where the ocean meets land, surfing the waves in a cedar canoe is an ancestral way of life that is now also a traditional sport. A feast for her family involves much the same as us Interior people, but with the riches of the ocean. The ocean provides a variety of oysters, clams, scallops, shrimp, crabs, octopus, halibut, eulachon, whale, seaweed, and all types of salmon and saltwater fish.

Tmíxʷ is a weaving of land, ocean, and sky; a weaving of energy, heartbeats, perseverance, and breath. Tmíxʷ is a weaving of shadows, mountain spirits, and songs. Tmíxʷ is a weaving of ancestral determination and fortitude, narratives echoing from sand, stones, and rock faces of ten million waterways. If tmíxʷ is listening, it will hear our hearts singing with the echoes of ancestral voices, our footsteps walking the paths they set in the most reverent way possible. Our voices might be nothing but gentle echoes of their teachings, our tears echoing their sorrow, our love as vast as the lands travelled by foot, canoe, and horseback all across tmíxʷ. If we also are tmíxʷ then we are temexw. We are, then, a weaving of light and DNA, stone and flesh, an embodiment of land and water.

We are our ancestors' prayers come to life.
We must follow this path, no matter how hard it gets.

If our ancestors are listening, they will hear us: hearts, minds, spirits, and bodies. Relearning ancestral languages, singing ancestral songs. Returning to ourselves. Here we are; we are coming now. We are the mothers of the next generation.

for the women who took us
within their circle of love,
mothers, aunties, grandmothers.

for the determination of
fathers, uncles, and grandfathers.

the caregivers

who adopted us, raised us, fought for us,
trained us to laugh wildly,
to have dedication and work hard
to achieve our goals and survive.

for those who truly cared
for the well-being of
all children,
not just their own.

we carry
courage in our hearts,
remembering their back-breaking struggle
to overcome their trauma
despite isolation, despite grief.

for them, with love
we rise

For the mothers, the sisters, the aunties, the fathers and uncles, the daughters and sons, the babies who disappeared and who didn't survive. All our LGBTQ2S+ Loved Ones who inspire us to have the courage to stand in our truth. Who inspire us to do better as parents. To have patience and endurance. To accept our wrongs and make things right.

And we watch her grace the floor with her strength. No shame veiling the beauty that exists within. If we could see her ancestors, Grandmothers and Grandfathers would be all around guiding her path. But we don't see that with our human eyes. All we see is the path. And all of us, coming along behind. In spirit form. In human form. We rise. We gather. As sisters, we sing.

She didn't get there by giving up. She did it, arrived at her destination, by hitting back. Paddling harder, getting up and going for that run to brush off the cobwebs, regardless of physical exhaustion. Her "ride or die" was no one else, no matter the pain. No matter the darkness. No matter how deep the trauma or triggers. No matter how powerless she felt at times, as she learned to let go of the hurt and keep pushing forward. Ten thousand days flopped out in ten thousand different ways. After being beaten. After being murdered. After being shattered by words and deeds. She rose up and prayed to her ancestors. She woke up and fed the children. She rose up, gathered herself, went to the water to bathe and to pray for herself, for her sons and daughters, and for future generations. She rose up again, every day. She rose up, choosing instead to ride the waves.

—

The sunlight reflects like a kaleidoscope off the enormous, iridescently clear lake. Canoes line the beach at Harrison Hot Springs from one end to the other. Saturday is race day. Usually this small town is overrun by tourists attracted to the huge glacier-fed, ice-cold, clear-blue lake and Sasquatch Provincial Park. However, on this day, the town awakens to the sound of Sts'ailes hand drums. Children, youth, Elders, and Sts'ailes community representatives are wearing sacred regalia and share traditional welcoming protocol with visitors to their territory. Harrison Hot Springs, the village, is overcome by xwelmexw, the original people of the land. Their DNA is ancient and deeply intertwined, rooted within s'ólh témexw. If xwelmexw had gathered in this same location hundreds of years ago, they would have travelled the Harrison River by canoe. Today, when the people arrive, their cedar race canoes are strategically bound to canoe racks on top of their vehicles.

Sts'ailes songs, dances, and stories acknowledge an ancient belonging to the tremendous lake and mountains surrounding Harrison Hot Springs. Voices singing to the land—woven with the breath of ancestors—rise up into the universe and echo through the town. This is the opening ceremony of the annual Sasquatch Days festival. A weekend of celebration, with the main activity being traditional cedar canoe racing with competitors from all age categories of Indigenous children, youth, and adults.

Depending on which race weekend it is and who is hosting, the children's, or "buckskins" categories generally start on the Friday, in the late afternoon. Singles, doubles, sixes, and elevens. Long days training on fresh and salt water have everyone tanned dark. They're all lean from summer days running around, playing on shore, and canoe racing. Aside from marathon race specials, the first races on Saturday and Sunday morning are set aside for the children. The water and wind conditions are usually calmer in the morning. It is incredible to see the kids' courage and strength develop, particularly as they learn to work together on the water. They become stronger and stronger through paddling and learning to steer their own small canoes. Paddling is not just a challenging sport; it is a way of life.

On the water, race after race, we see a display of empowerment. Joy in the sunshine is reflected in the faces of children, on all the crews on the water. Cedar canoes line the main waterfront from one end all the way to the other. Tents, big canoes, small canoes, xwelmexw tanned all shades of brown, all ages engaged in their favourite race of the year. Indigenous bodies and Indigenous voices lifted in the calling of switches and cheering from the beach. Strength expressed through proficiency and the ability to ride the water regardless of the weather. There have been days when the wind brings rough water and even monsoon-like rainstorms. As a lake race, the one thing we never have to be concerned about is the ever-changing ocean tides.

Every weekend, the canoes travel from one location to the next. Every race weekend, the beach we inhabit becomes home. Fresh water, salt water, every weekend the canoes line the beaches. Alive like great cedar beings, the canoes dance and sing upon the waves.

In the weeks following that particular Sasquatch Days festival, there are online displays of empowered children and youth, families, Sts'ailes and Stó:lō community members. Far and wide across tmíxʷ-Turtle Island images are shared of empowered Indigenous children, families, and canoe clubs, including on social media throughout the Fraser Valley, Chilliwack, and Harrison Hot Springs. The strength, power, and beauty of Sts'ailes, Stó:lō, and other Coast Salish paddlers is absolutely breathtaking.

There is no way to prepare for the backlash of racist commentary from certain local Harrison community members. People of all backgrounds come out to support and to enjoy the races. However, the words are shocking. They are hurtful. They are visceral. To step back and have grace during difficult times, to not waste precious energy on those who spread hate and online vitriol is challenging. The ones who carry hatred do not see or recognize how important the beautiful empowerment of Indigenous children and communities is.

Maybe they felt it. The powerful and ancient energy of a people who belong so deeply, they are a weaving of land, life force, and water. Perhaps this kind of ancestral interconnectedness and interrelatedness is scary for those who are so disconnected? What exists on these beaches uplifts the hearts, minds, spirits of the people, starting from childhood and continuing right into Elderhood. At one time it was specifically for transportation and harvesting food; now it is a sport that requires tremendous dedication as well as mental and physical strength.

—

Reweaving self and community takes so many forms. Listening deeply to the words and embodied knowledge of Elders and Knowledge Carriers. We are continuously disentangling ourselves from generations of racism, colonial violence, and genocide. The hurt is tangible; it is unquestionable. It is generational. Reweaving ourselves takes time. The sorrow has been woven into our existence for too long. In order to show younger generations how to transcend a history of pain, we need to do more than break a trail. We must mark the path travelled for those who do not know the way.

The creative work of Indigenous storytellers has inspired me to try harder and dig deeper into my cultural roots and knowledge as an Indigenous writer, as a human being, and as a mother. The work of Leanne Betasamosake Simpson, such as *Dancing on Our Turtle's Back*, is one narrative I reflect on over and over again. She describes the concept of resurgence and why it is important for us as Indigenous people; she encourages us to "move ourselves beyond resistance and survival, to flourishment and mino bimaadiziwin."[1] The online version of the *Oxford English Dictionary* explains resurgence as "[t]he action or an act of rising again (chiefly in *fig.* senses)."[2] Through community work and interactions with friends, Loved Ones, and families, we create a path of resurgence and mino bimaadiziwin so that it's normal for everyone. We can reclaim that understanding of ourselves as an empowered people. And so our task is to make each day an example of flourishing within abundant and empowered lives, in such a way that Loved Ones all around us also feel uplifted and inspired.

Simpson talks about an event in her traditional territory where the people celebrated on the city streets, and how it felt to celebrate so openly, in a place where she had experienced and witnessed systemic racism throughout her life. During the Idle No More movement, surrounded by our Elders, we took over the streets of the Nicola Valley. I helped organize a rally for the continued protection of the ten thousand waterways in our valley. People of all

---

1 Leanne Betasamosake Simpson, *Dancing on Our Turtle's Back: Stories of Nishnaabeg Re-Creation, Resurgence, and a New Emergence*, (Winnipeg: ARP Books, 2011), 17.

2 *Oxford English Dictionary*, s.v. "resurgence," last modified September 2010, http://www.oed.com/view/Entry/164095.

ages participated on foot, and those who couldn't walk travelled in vehicles. Many of us carried signs and sang with hand drums for the Idle No More events in the city of Merritt. People on horseback rode in from one of the reserves outside of town, and together riders and walkers marched down the streets and had a drumming circle at one of the intersections. I remember experiencing pride, love, and belonging, as well as moments of remembered hurt, shame, and fear. Courage kept us strong as we walked among our Elders. These events occurred simultaneously all across Canada, and I wondered, did everyone across Canada struggle to untangle those same feelings?

"We are not shameful people. We have done nothing wrong."[3] Powerful statements of truth spoken by the Elders who guide Leanne Betasamosake Simpson. Those words guide me like a beacon. They remind me to be courageous. They affirm the work we are doing. They remind me we have every right to fight for what is sacred to us, for the future well-being of our children.

Across Canada, the state of well-being is not consistent; it goes up and down like waves. Following the seasons, because each season has its tasks. Come springtime, we begin harvesting again, which is one way of reconnecting with our Elders and children. And now, due to COVID-19 lockdowns, our cultural existence has switched to an online experience of winter song gatherings and prayers. We strive to take care of heart, mind, and spirit despite the pandemic.

To be good mothers. To be patient fathers. To be loving parents. We learn to be empowered human beings, so that we can raise

---

3 Betasamosake Simpson, *Dancing on Our Turtle's Back*, 14.

empowered human beings. When we fall, to remind ourselves that it is okay. It's okay to fall. Then we must rise again, dust ourselves off, and get back on the trail.

Early adulthood, childhood, and youth swept by so quickly. I am now a grown woman entering my middle years. And, I am still so clumsy at life. But I am trying. As a woman I allow myself to be all of it. To rage. To hurt. To be uncouth. To be messy. To be weak and experience grief. To face trauma and betrayal and to rise.

With every stage of putting together this collection, I have been afraid. As each word landed on the page, I stopped to reflect. I put it away, I brought it back. My auntie said, "Stories are like grandmothers coming to your door to visit. If you leave them uncared for, they will only wait for so long."

Reweave the Universe

I recall a moment in deep winter when snow was heavy on the ground, following a night of prayerful songs. As I sat with my Elder, I spoke in reflection about the cyclical direction in which many of our most sacred ceremonies proceed, all across tmíxʷ. A timeless moment passed, as my dear Elder paused in contemplation. "We go in one direction to untangle ourselves, and then afterwards, we return to our path and start again."

Working on my doctoral research and dissertation, I continuously weave back and forth between scholarly thought and deep reflection on the stories and teachings of my Elders. Scholarly thought is not a natural process for me. In her foreword to the second edition of *Decolonizing Methodologies*, Māori scholar, Linda Tuhiwai Smith states,

> This book explores the intersection of two powerful worlds, the world of Indigenous peoples and the world of research. They are two important worlds for me: I move within them; in one sense I was born into one and educated into the other. I negotiate the intersection of these worlds every day.[1]

Writing for the university causes me significant anxiety because of the racism and discrimination that I have often experienced in

---

1 Linda Tuhiwai Smith, *Decolonizing Methodologies: Research and Indigenous Peoples*, 2nd ed. (London: Zed Books, 2012), ix.

educational settings since I was a child. I am also afraid of failure, or worse, disappointing my Elders. Self-doubt and low self-worth no longer have a place, yet they continue to try to claim space within me. As a writer and a mother, what I am more afraid of is stopping. It is important to keep moving forward.

Someone once asked me, "What makes you feel more grounded and connected: the water or the land?" Truly the water and the land are each intertwined with the places that are most accepting and peaceful. In her doctoral dissertation, "Constructing Indigeneity," Dr. Jeannette Armstrong, a fluent speaker of Nsyílxcn, explains the complexities of translating the word tmíxʷ as, "the state of humans being intertwined and bound with the tmíxʷ as one unified strand."[2] A weaving of all living things: human, animals, plants, and all life forces across the land—this is my understanding. Tmíxʷ, meditating on and weaving this translation together with my learnings from the work of Leanne Betasamosake Simpson and other Indigenous writers who actively speak about resurgence, has become a deeply complex and fundamental strand in understanding my personal journey towards reawakening what has been sleeping and healing what was broken.

Armstrong's interpretation notes "human existence within nature as life-force." She describes how the "image of twisting many strands into one as in a rope and coiling around and around invokes the concept of nature. It invokes the image of the animals,

---

2 Jeannette Christine Armstrong, "Constructing Indigeneity: Syilx Okanagan Oraliture and tmixʷcentrism " (PhD diss., Greifswald Universitätsbibliothek, 2010), 159.

plants, fish, birds, reptiles and insects, being pulled from the fanning outward around the human being into a single cord with the human, coiled year upon year."[3] The word tmíxʷ is used in both Nsyílxcn and Nłeʔkepmxcín. Temexw and sʼólh témexw translate as "land," and "our world, our land" in Halqʼeméylem. There is a deeper and more dynamic interpretation of these Halqʼeméylem words; however, I do not carry this knowledge. This reciprocal interconnectedness with tmíxʷ is essential to everything we are as Indigenous people, and from this relationship comes true belonging.

When I contemplate the weaving of tmíxʷ with concepts of resurgence, a sequence of significant memories pass through my mind. I ponder the ways our Interior and Coastal Salish languages have such dynamic variations and similarities, such as the words tmíxʷ, temexw, temxulaxʷ, temíxw. Who we are, who we were, what will always be, and what we will become. The strands described by Armstrong in her detailed translation have become a weaving of words, images, and significant moments, of ways of being and of how, as a people, we continue to live reciprocally through ancestral teachings and within our sacred lands.

In ceremony we are reminded how to be humble and silent. Sit with the ones we trust to give guidance—our Elders, Loved Ones—and listen to their teachings, songs, and prayers. Learning to have reverence for all living things and to pray the way our Elders have taught us is one stage of coming to our senses. When the ceremony is over and the work is complete, we start our daily

---

3 Armstrong, "Constructing Indigeneity"

lives again, renewed. With each new step, the teachings we have gained guide us. To do better. To live in a good way. To have courage and endurance to do the work we need to do. Crawl inside the kwílstn, the womb of tmíxʷ with our hands empty aside from humble offerings to feed the spirit. We bring nothing but our human selves, our spiritual selves. Sit in darkness on fragrant fir boughs as the steam from the merímstn, medicine water and smoke from the sage, surround us. A safe place to pray, to heal, and to humbly exist in the presence of our ancestors when they arrive—because there is always that moment in ceremony when the ancestors walk in. And that moment is tremendous and beautiful. Take time to put mind, body, and spirit back together. Remember how it feels to have nothing but the Creator and the good teachings of our most trusted Elders and Knowledge Carriers.

In another sequence of memories, tmíxʷ is awake with springtime growth, green leaves emerging from the Southern Interior yellows and browns. The sun is shining as a springtime breeze swirls gently around us. We park the car and walk across the train bridge. My auntie with her bingo hat on and hair tied back: not yet an Elder but approaching Elderhood with gentle grace. Me as a young woman in my early twenties. Both of us wearing good shoes and long pants. A mixture of english and Nłeʔkepmxcín falls from her mouth with a distinct lisp. She laughs often because within tmíxʷ, she is confident and in her happy place. The only sounds we hear aside from our voices talking and laughing are the occasional eagle call, the birds diving and singing all around us, and the buzz of awakened bees and yellow-jacket wasps.

Raised by her grandmother, my auntie didn't attend Indian Residential School. She is a tremendously humble Knowledge

Carrier of plants with a great sense of humour. This was one of our many harvesting excursions. We had travelled from Shulus Reserve in Scwéxmxuym̓xʷ, north along Highway 8 towards Spences Bridge to a place she referred to as Dot—one of her favourite locations—to harvest spécn̓. She took time to acknowledge the identifying features and explain what it was used for. She taught me the name spécn̓. Afterwards, I learned that in english, it is referred to as Indian hemp or dogbane. She uprooted it from the ground, quickly cleaning it. The harvest and preparation is an important element of her teaching. Her strong hands moved through each step quickly. Then using her lap, she quickly spun and twined the spécn̓. Her process of actively teaching was so efficient; I was astounded by the length and strength of her rope when she completed her demonstration. I felt qʷənqʷént, slightly pitiful, because my clumsy hands did not have the skill. Time spent upon tmíxʷ with one of my dear aunties is always peaceful and healing. Although I have nowhere near the same level of mastery that she has achieved, the merímstn is in twining together of stories and moments through harvesting and time on tmíxʷ.

The sky is grey and slightly overcast, and there is heavy moisture in the air; however, so far, there has been no rain for our drive into the mountains. S'ólh témexw, this earth right here is home. Sts'iyó ye smesti'yexw slhá:li, she exits the car, a wolf but not, fiercely ethereal emerging from her den. She deeply inhales and then exhales with the land. She fluidly walks into a tall stand of cedars. Absolutely confident in her safe space, the tall length of her momentarily disappears then appears again within the trees. Temexw is awakening to another springtime, the embrace of new plants emerging. Their branches reach out, brushing the weight of daily life from our bodies. Tremendous ancestral cedars observing, recognizing, and rejoicing in the embrace of spirit and spirit. Cedar beings dance and we are surrounded by a vibration of heartbeats. With heart, mind, and spirit she is the embodiment of transformation, more than a woman, more than a man. Sts'iyó ye smesti'yexw slhá:li. Twin-Spirited woman, femininity. Loved, cherished, ancestral, there is an awakening with her sacred emergence, and this journey has been complex, dynamic, multi-faceted. The part of her that's risen, the part of her that's burned, the part of her that's reawakened. She is fire, but she is not. She is wind, and so much more. She is water when it rages, but also when it's peaceful, currents continuous, warm in the summer with cold far beneath. She is a weaving of all things born and made of the land. This journey to her true identity has not been easy.

Touching each tree with gentle reverence as she passes, examining root systems, requesting permission to harvest. True love and acceptance is fundamental and at that reciprocal moment when consent is granted, she reaches deep within. Her hand disappears as though diving into the heart of the tree, emerging with a coursing vessel of life. A root from the cedar tree. Sacred words of prayer and honour spoken, she pulls it free then swiftly ties it around her waist. There is an energy with union: Cedar recognizes cedar. Sts'iyó ye smesti'yexw slhá:li. Her weaving hands guided by the universe. Weaver heart pulled apart and put back together, mentored then covered with the true love of her Grandmother. The ancestors gather and embrace her, lift her when she falters, when she falls. She rises, again and again.

Sts'iyó ye smesti'yexw slhá:li. The Twin-Spirited Loved Ones. If we call ourselves allies, we must stand by and protect. With hands,

feet, voices. Love was the first thing taken away by the colonizers and Indian Residential Schools, replaced with hurt and shame.
Love must come first for ourselves, our Loved Ones, and younger
generations no matter what. When Loved Ones come forward and
identify as LGBTQ2S+, loving them unconditionally is of utmost
importance, so they understand how valued and important they
truly are.

Xʼúʔ sqáyxcín—the language of the original people. Xwelmexw—
the original people, of this temexw, tmíxʷ. One strand in the sacred
weaving of land and waterscape, of all things. Standing among
cedars with my Stó:lō sister, existing within Stó:lō temexw, woven
among all the sacred strands of dynamic energy, existence, fibres,
and matter.

An old-style wooden spindle whorl is set up inside the band
hall. Coast Salish ladies and matriarchs gather inside. Some are
sitting and knitting; others are preparing to learn to weave. Large
and small weaving frames are set up, in different stages of completion. With confident hands, an Elder examines a bag of raw
wool that she has been saving for this day. She draws on the raw
woollen thread, tenderly, continuously. Making the strands some-
what uniform. She prepares to spin, and everyone gathers around
to watch. Spinning and twining and then weaving. Weaving their
dreams. Weaving together the stories of how grandmothers taught
their grandchildren. Weaving together stories of harvest, tufts of
raw, mountain-goat wool from Lhílhequay, Mt. Cheam. Reweaving
together stories of strength: hearts, spirits, minds, and bodies. Each
individual careful to keep a clear, joy-filled, and peaceful mind as
they work to reweave the universe.

Valley to valley, here in British Columbia, as the original people of these lands, we are tmíxʷ because we are intertwined and interconnected much like the river systems and waterways, like the trees that have sustained our ancestors since time beyond memory. One day our voices, our breath, our dust will become tmíxʷ too. Still here, yet with a changed form. What endures are the vibrations of ancestors all across Indigenous land. Ancient burials on mountain sides, ancient villages, walking trails, and the awakened pulse of ancestral spirits. To have the gift and the burden of connection to the ancestors is to carry the sacred knowledge and discipline of ancestral teachings. As human beings, as ƛ'úʔ sqáyx, as xwelmexw, as the original people. Our awareness of the ancestral village sites and sentient beings reminds us to stand deeply embedded within and empowered by our culture.

Witnesses. We are the ones who must not falter. True love and integrity must come first. Reweave the universe. It is time; it is time for the gatherers to arrive, for harvest. For the singers to sing the songs of transformation. For the storytellers to tell the stories of resurgence. It is time to reweave the universe, to weave ourselves anew. Convey stories, manifest dreams, weave hearts, families, spirits back together.

Offering

on this page I place berries
round like the belly
of our human mother and earth mother.
round like the lodge, like the womb that carried and birthed us
round like the cycle of our existence
from spirit to birth and infancy into childhood,
puberty, adolescence, adulthood, Elderhood,
returning full circle back to the spirit.

on this page I place
the rooted ones who weave us to the land,
the ones that nourish all beings
with lifeblood flowing in their veins.

on this page I place the most sacred finned swimmers & winged ones
those who honour the water and those who honour the sky
with their existence. they each give their lives to nourish us all.

on this page I place the four-legged ones: deer, moose, elk.
those that offer their bodies
to nourish the bellies of our ancestors and us.

on this page I place water
that nourishes all things.
our revered children and Elders, us.
our beloved rooted ones, berries, plants, and mlámn,
those with four legs, those with two legs, the finned swimmers,
    and those with wings.
the water that has been our place to pray, our place to play and our
    place to bathe.

since the beginning of remembered time,
since before the time the first human came to be.
since the time the first human walked this earth
speaking fluently as Loved Ones.
with all living things.

spíləx̣m
this humble offering to the ancestors,
the good Grandmothers and good Grandfathers.
it is a prayer for well-being, for sustenance, for endurance to carry on.
grateful.

on this page, I offer
simple words. narratives.
spíləx̣m.
placed together as lived memories.
reflections, meditations, fragments,
too many puzzles,
trying to find a way back to being whole.
pieces of the original weavings
leading to a better tomorrow.
not trying to return to an idealized pre-colonial life,
finding balance, amidst the gifts and trials.

on this page I offer
prayers, fears, rage, courage, love
moments of joy and tears like the falling
of many-faceted raindrops
striving to see every shimmering light.

on this page I offer
remembered teachings
spoken not by me but by my Elders
some when I was small, some when I was tall
some while healing from the most shattered stages of grief
some when I was confused about which path to follow, step by step.

she braids a story.
yes, she does, she weaves a story.
pulls together strands,
woven words. some bring us round and round,
back to the beginning again.

she pulls out the rot. pulls out the breakage.
removes the decay
sorting. rearranging. composting
hunts, gathers for pieces to remind us, every day,
what it feels like to be whole.

we are the ones.
our children are the ones.
our grandchildren are the ones
our ancestors prayed for. persevered for.

pause now,
have patience
within the silence
the full, aching silence
with heart mind body spirit
hear the words of our Elders.
patient, the way we were taught.
wait to hear their breath embodied
within the breath of our children as they play.

Acknowledgements

My heartfelt gratitude to:

My entire family, my Elders, and my Loved Ones.

Kʷuʷscémxʷ and special acknowledgements to Sharon and David Antoine, Marty Aspinall, Deanna Francis, Xiquelum Gene Harry, Scotty and Carol Holmes, Mandy Jimmie, Helen and Herb Joe, Siyámíya Diana Kay, Mary and Ed Louie, Naxaxalhts'i Dr. Sonny McHalsie, Brian and Kowaintco Michel, Garry Thomas Morse, Alayna Munce, Isaac Murdoch, Ray Natraoro, uncle and Grand Chief Kat and Nancy Pennier, Chief Mark Point, The Honourable Dr. Steven and Dr. Gwen Point, Gail Point, Thet-simiya Wendy Ritchie, Sk̓ʷóz Delia Shuter, Nelson Stewart Jr., and Saylesh Wesley, as well as HighWater Press.

MFA Graduate Supervisor, Keith Maillard and PhD Supervisory Committee: Dr. Jeannette Armstrong, Dr. Bill Cohen, Dr. Allison Hargreaves, and the late Dr. Greg Younging.

Kʷukʷscémxʷ for the courage, Auntie Maria Campbell.

Glossary

Indigenous Peoples and Languages

The Nations, peoples, and languages in this glossary are only those mentioned in this book. There are many, many others, both in British Columbia and across what is now Canada.

Anishinaabe	people who speak Anishinaabemowin; traditional homelands include and radiate out from the Great Lakes region
Athapaskan	people also known as Athabaskan or Dene; traditional homelands in the northern regions of BC and Canada
Dakelh	the People Who Travel Upon Water; also known as Nak'azdli or Carrier
Danezāgé'	Kaska or Kaska Dene
Dene-Zaa	Peace River region of BC
Diiʔdiitidq	Ditidaht
Éy7á7juuthem	Comox
Gitxsanimx̱	language spoken by the Gitxsan
Haíłzaqv	Heilsuk
Halq'eméylem	language spoken in the Fraser Valley spoken by the People of the River
Hǝńq'ǝmińǝm'	spoken on the coastal mainland closer to the mouth of the Fraser River and by the Xʷmǝθkʷǝy'ǝm
Hul'q'umi'num	language spoken by Coast Salish people on Vancouver Island
Ktunaxa	Kutenai
Kwakwa̱ka̱'wakw	the people who speak Kwak'wala

— 314 —

Lílwat	Lílwat Nation, Interior Salish; part of the St̓át̓yemc Nations
Ɫingít	Tlinqit
Lummi	Coast Salish people
Métis	a very specific and distinct group of people who can trace their lineage to the intermarriages between Indigenous women and the original fur traders at the time of contact
Michif	Métis language
Nedu'ten	language spoken by Lake Babine Nation
Nisga'a	Nisga'a
Nɬeʔkepmx	previously known as Thompson River Salish people
Nɬeʔkepmxcín	language spoken by the Nɬeʔkepmx
Nsyílxcn	language spoken by the Syílx people
Nuučaańuɬ	Nuu-chah-nulth
Nuxalkmc	Nuxalk ˈˈ
Quw'utsun	Cowichan
Scẃéxmx	"People of the Creeks"; Nɬeʔkepmx of the Nicola Valley
Scẃéxmxuyṁxʷ	territory of the People of the Creeks
Secwepemctsín	language spoken by the Secwepmx
Secwepmx	Secwepmc
SenćoTen	Language of the Saanich people
Sgüüx̱s	Klemtu
She shashishalhem	language spoken by the Sechelt
Sḵwx̱wú7mesh sníchim	language spoken by the Squamish Nation
Sḵwx̱wú7mesh Úxwumixw	Squamish Nation ("village")
Sƛ'aƛ'imx / Stát̓imcets	Lillooet Nation, language, and people
Sṁalgyax̱	Tsimshian

Stát̕yemc	The Stát̕yemc Nations inhabit the territories throughout Lillooet, Pemberton, Bridge River, Mount Currie, British Columbia.
Stó:lō	People of the River
Sts'ailes	Chehalis
Syílx	Okanagan Interior Salish people
Tāɬtān	Tahltan
Tla'amin	formerly Sliammon
Tse'khene	formerly Sekani
Tsilhqot'in	People of the River (formerly Chilcotin)
Tsleil-Waututh	People of the Inlet (Burrard Inlet)
Tutchone	Northern Tutchone
Wetalh	Wetalh
Wit'suwit'en	Wet'suwet'en
Wuikinuxv	Oweekeeno – Rivers Inlet, formerly Oweekeeno Nation
Xa"islakala	Haisla
X̲aaydaa Kil	Haida
Xʷməθkʷəy'əm	Musqueam; people who speak Həńq'əmińəm

Halq'eméylem Words and Phrases

Chiyo:m	Cheam, a community in Stó:lō temexw
ísala?	two
Lhílhequay	Mount Cheam
nec'e	one
Sema:th Lake	Sumas Lake
s'ólh témexw	our land, our world
Sqew'qeyl	Skowkale, a community in Stó:lō temexw
sqwélqwel	remembered stories

Sts'iyó ye smesti'yexw slhá:li	Twin-Spirited woman
Stó:lō temexw	traditional territory of the People of the River
temexw	land
tomiyeqw	"great-great-great-great grandparents and great-great-great-great grandchildren"
xwelmexw	people of the s'ólh témexw

Nsyílxcn Words and Phrases

kwílstn	sweatlodge
kwulencuten	Creator, Great Spirit
merímstn	medicine
síya	saskatoon berries
sn'ix'wam	Medicine Dance, winter dance
Spaxomin	Upper Nicola Indian Reserve and place name
spíƛ'm	bitterroot
temxulaxʷ	land

Nłeʔkepmxcín Words and Phrases

ćéłt	cold
ćewéteʔ	wild celery
cɔceʔ	younger sister
ćəlćále	black huckleberries
ćəłetkʷu	"Coldwater" place name
ćuwenéy̓tmx	sasquatch
k̓éceʔ	Labrador tea, also called "Indian tea," trapper's tea, and swamp tea
keʔłés	three
kʷátłp	cedar

k̓ʷməm'iʔmeʔ	little, small
kʷuʷscémxʷ	thank you
kx̌éʔ	grandmother
łəʔpnteʔ	oyster mushrooms
łk̓ʷəpn	bitterroot
ƛ̓úʔ sqáyx	the original people
ƛ̓úʔ sqáyxcín	language of the original people
mlámn	medicine
mús	four
nám̓ ʔesx̌ʷəzcín	I love you with all my heart
nkéxʷ	bitter pudding—traditional dessert
Nwéyc	"Nooaitch" place name
péłuskʷu	lake
p̓ésk̓eʔ	hummingbird
péłec	a wake or memorial honouring a deceased Loved One
péyeʔ	one
p̓əp̓éy̓łe	frog
p̓w'əm	fart
qálex̣	digging stick
qʷənqʷént	pitiful
qʷuʔ	water
scáqʷm	saskatoon berries
scmém'iʔt	children
Séwtaʔ/Shuta	family name (anglicized as Shuter)
séyeʔ	two
seytknmx	the people
səxʷsúxʷ	grizzly bear
Shulus (sulús)	anglicized place name

sínci?	younger brother
skíxze?	mother
sk̓epy̓éɬp	wild rose bush
sk̓ʷóz	term for aunt or grand-aunt
smíycuy	deer meat
snúṅk̓ʷe	friends
spápze?	grandfather
sp̓éčn	Indian hemp or dogbane
spé?ec	bear
spíləx̣m	remembered stories, moccasin telegraph, or news
Sptétkʷ	"Springs" place name
spték̓ʷɬ	stories from the time of talking animals
spzúz'u?	birds
sqáyxʷ	man
sqyéytn	salmon
sxeṅx	stone
sxéxeṅx	little rocks
Sxéxeṅx	"Little Rocks" place name (Shackan Indian Band)
sx̣ʷúsm	soap berries; the whipped ice cream made from soap berries
synk̓y̓ép	coyote; also Coyote from spték̓ʷɬ
s?é?e?	crow or crows
s?ístkn	winter home or pit house (used by Interior Salish peoples)
tətúwṅ	wild potatoes, also known as western spring beauty
tmíxʷ	land (see also page 301)

wík'ne ł súsəkʷlíʔ	"I see [jesus] [the Creator]." Note: I am not sure of the exact translation for "súsəkʷlíʔ" the Elders' Meadowlark song. The "concept of jesus" would have been introduced through colonization and Indian Residential Schools, but the word existed before that. In my interpretation, I visualized the sacred holy spirit as alive in all things all across tmíxʷ.
yémit	pray
yémxne	someone is praying for someone or something
yémxne e qʷuʔ	pray for the water
yémxne e tmíxʷ	pray for the land
yéyeʔ	grandmother
yúxkn	storage shed
zəlkʷúʔ	chokecherries
ʔímc	grandchild
ʔíṁec	grandchildren

Other Words and Phrases

bakwam	the original people (Kwak'wala language)
mino bimaadiziwin	the good life (Anishinaabemowin language)
Mooshoom	Grandfather (Cree and Michif languages)
mush	a porridge; word used among many Indian Residential School survivors across Canada for oatmeal
temíxw	land (Sk̲w̲xwú7mesh sníchim)

Index

dogbane. *See* spéċn
Douglas Lake, 138
Douglas Lake Cattle Company, 139–40
Dumont, Gabriel, 47, 112
Dumont, Isadore, 112

eagles, 89, 119, 159, 303; feathers, 101, 288
East Hastings Street, Vancouver, 275–76
Edmonton, 88
Edmonton Friendship Centre, 24
Elders; and BC Elders Gathering, 191, 249, 259–60; and ceremony and prayer, 114, 129, 247–48, 287–89, 293, 302–3; gathering and preparation of traditional foods, 64, 97; and language, 97, 104, 138–39, 147, 183, 209, 277; and residential schools, 125–27, 135, 148–49, 192–93; and stories and teachings, 21, 24, 32, 103–7, 123, 137, 143–45, 150, 152, 184, 185, 188, 208, 228, 248–50, 266–67, 278–79, 284–85, 296, 300, 303, 310–11
elementary school, 61, 66, 68, 126, 136, 182, 187, 188, 208
elk, 88, 308
Éy7á7juuthem, 133, 314

fir, 51, 103, 155, 159, 266, 275; boughs, 11, 101, 128, 211, 235, 239, 248, 288, 303
fireweed, 62, 209
fishing, 46, 86, 97, 128, 121, 143, 144, 149, 210. *See also* salmon
Fish Lake, 28, 85, 138, 152, 215
foster care, 39, 78, 87, 93–94, 148, 264, 289. *See also* Indian Residential Schools; Sixties Scoop

Fraser Canyon, 28, 139, 144–45, 149
Fraser River, 123, 137, 144–45, 149–50, 208, 249, 257
Freshie, 12
fried bologna and rice, 12
frogs. *See* p̓əp̓éy̓łe
fruit-picking, 145–46, 171
fry bread, 12

genocide, 107, 141, 262, 263–64, 296–97. *See also* disease; disenfranchisement; Indian Act; Indian Residential School
Gitxsan, 314
Gitxsanimx̱ (language spoken by the Gitxsan), 133
godmom, 4, 15–18, 21–22, 23, 25, 76–77, 89, 94, 97, 128, 145, 150, 152, 171, 192–95, 213, 281, 289; grief over death of children, 90, 220; illness and death of, 18, 188, 220–34, 242–46, 247
Grand-Auntie Elizabeth, 85
Grand-Uncle Edward, 85
Grandpa Adam, 19, 33, 36, 38, 66, 75, 181, 244, 248; and residential school, 39
grief, 51, 99, 107, 167–96, 199, 211, 241–50, 252, 260, 261–71, 280, 281, 286, 292, 299, 310. *See also* sorrow; trauma
grizzly bears. *See* səx̌ʷsúxʷ

Haida Gwaii, 136, 146
Haíɫzaqv, 133, 151, 314
Halq'eméylem, 123, 125–26, 133, 288, 314
hamburger stew, 19–20
Hannah, Darwin, and Mamie Henry, 144
Harrison Hot Springs, British Columbia, 293–94, 295–96
harvesting huckleberries, 33–35, 36

Hay, Louise, 182
healing. *See* canoe racing; ceremony; Elders; hiking; medicines; medicine wheel; prayer; running; sweatlodges
Hedley, 28
Hən̓q̓əmin̓əm̓, 123, 133, 288, 314
hides, soaking and tanning, 12, 27
high school, 61, 66, 89–90, 94, 95, 126, 136, 182, 188
hiking, 100, 199, 200, 210, 281
hops, 145, 146
hospitals, 53–55, 124–25
huckleberries. *See* ċəlċále
Hudson Bay, Saskatchewan, 5
Hul'q'umi'num, 123, 133, 314
hummingbirds. *See* p̓éske?
hunting, 5, 25–26, 86

Idle No More movement, 297
Indian Act, 85–86, 137
Indian Agents, 139
Indian Bands, 137
Indian Friendship Centres, 24, 88–89, 94, 95, 266
Indian hemp. *See* spéċn
Indian ice cream. *See* sx̌ʷúsm
Indian National Finals Rodeo (Albuquerque, New Mexico), 81–82
Indian paintbrush, 62, 209
Indian Reserves, 24–25, 137–38, 140, 149, 264. *See also* disenfranchisement; off-reserve; Indian status
Indian Residential Schools, 38–39, 87, 124, 125–27, 192–93, 306, 320; graveyards at, 126, 148, 150, 264, 265; intergenerational survivors of, 130, 148–49, 220, 245, 262–66, 283, 288, 289; and loss of languages and traditional names and knowledge,

Native rights movement, 24
Naxaxalhts'i, 149
Nedu'ten, 133, 315
Nicola Lake, 138, 152, 249
Nicola River, 137–38, 257
Nicola Tribal Association, 123
Nicola Valley, 28, 64, 65, 68, 78, 137–39, 143, 144, 148, 152, 185, 211, 297, 304
Nicola Valley Elders' Group, 277
Nicola Valley Institute of Technology, 63, 123, 126–27
Nisga'a, 133, 151, 315
nkéxʷ (bitter pudding—traditional dessert), 118, 236, 318
Nłeʔkepmx (Thompson River Salish people), 11, 28, 55, 78, 94, 115, 137, 139, 185, 208, 217, 229, 247, 250, 261, 277, 315. See also Nłeʔkepmxcín
Nłeʔkepmxcín (Nłeʔkepmx language), 21–22, 36, 63, 75, 80, 116, 123, 133, 138, 143, 228, 277, 288, 302, 303, 315
nodding onion, 64, 117
non-status, 24
"Nooaitch" Indian Reserve. See Nwéyc
Nsyílxcn (Syílx language) 20, 21–22, 36, 63, 85, 116, 133, 143, 138, 194, 228, 277, 301, 317
Nuučaańuł, 133, 315
Nuxalkmc, 133, 151, 315
Nwéyc ("Nooaitch" Indian Reserve), 14, 138, 318

ocean foods, 291
off-reserve, 25, 147
Ogopogo, 152
Okanagan Lake, 152
Okanagan speakers. See Syílx
Okanagan Valley, 97, 139, 144, 145–46, 152, 171–72
Oweekeeno, 133

P.A., 5, 6
parenting, 283–85
péłuskʷu (lake), 318
p'éskeʔ (hummingbird), 51, 62, 79, 318
péłec (a wake or memorial, honouring a deceased Loved One), 318
Pep, Great-Grandpa (Tim), 28
p̓əp̓éýłe (frog), 37, 119, 318
pine, 26, 31, 32, 70, 81, 103, 114, 117, 172, 185, 211; jack, 44, 116, 147; lodgepole, 275; needles, 105, 132, 151; ponderosa, 215
porcupines, 135–36, 152
potlatches, 144, 146
powwows, 172, 173, 175
prayer, 78–79, 97, 101–2, 106, 114–15, 139, 182, 184, 197, 210, 218, 228, 238, 239, 249, 257, 258, 259, 286–89, 302, 305, 309, 310. See also ceremony; sweatlodges
pregnancy, 76, 78–79
p̓w'əm (fart), 277, 278, 318

qálex (digging stick), 116, 318
qʷənqʷént (pitiful), 238, 304, 318
Querel Gravel & Lumber, 5, 6
Quilchena, 26, 84, 138, 195, 215, 220
Quw'utsun, 133, 165–66, 315

racism, 85, 98–100, 131, 295–97, 298, 300–301. See also disenfranchisement; Indian Act; Indian Residential Schools; language, loss of
rainbow trout, 140
rape, 66–67, 73, 93, 98
rattlesnakes, 119
red willow, 51
relocation, forcible, 86
reserves, 24–25, 85–86

residential schools. See Indian Residential Schools
resurgence, concept of, 296–97
Riel, Louis, 47, 112
rodeos, 16, 81–82, 145–46, 171, 220, 230
Royal Proclamation of 1763, 86
running as healing, 199–206, 281

sage, 114, 172, 239, 247, 257, 287, 288, 303
sagebrush, 11, 44, 151, 178, 214, 275
Salish, colonial origins of the term, 28, 137
salmon. See sqyéytn
Sardis, British Columbia, 124, 125, 142
Saskatchewan River, 7, 8, 47
saskatoon berries. See scáqʷm
Sasquatch Days Festival, Harrison Hot Springs, 294–96
scáqʷm (saskatoon berries), 51, 80, 94, 117, 208, 236, 318
scmém'iʔt (children), 33, 318
Scwéxmx (People of the Creeks), 11, 117, 137, 151, 258, 315
Scwéxmxuym̓xʷ (territory of the People of the Creeks), 304, 315
Secwepmc. See Secwepmx
Secwepmx, 114, 115, 138, 192, 193, 251, 261, 315. See also Secwepemctsín
Secwepemctsín (Secwepemc language), 133, 288, 315
Sema:th Lake, 316. See also Sumas Lake, draining of
SenćoTen, 133, 315
sewing, 5–6, 15–18, 32
Séwtaʔ (Shuta) (family name, anglicized as Shuter), 139, 318
seytknmx (the people), 34, 318